Graduate Women's Studies

Visions and Realities

*Papers arising from a Conference
held at York University May 1995*

**Edited by
Ann B. Shteir**

Inanna Publications and Education Inc.

Published by:
Inanna Publications and Education Inc.
operating as *Canadian Woman Studies/les cahiers de la femme*
212 Founders College, York University
4700 Keele Street
North York, Ontario
M3J 1P3

Printed and Bound in Canada
by University of Toronto Press, Inc.

Cover Art: Verna Linney, "Sapientia," Pastel, 52" x 36", 1992
Cover Design/Interior Design: Luciana Ricciutelli

The Graduate Programme in Women's Studies at York University
gratefully acknowledges the support of the
Social Sciences and Humanities Research Council, Ottawa, Canada.

Canadian Cataloguing in Publication Data

Main Entry under title:
Graduate women's studies: visions and realities:
papers arising from a conference held at York University May 1995

ISBN 0-9681290-0-5

1. Women's studies – Congresses. 2. Universities and colleges –
Graduate work – Congresses. I. Shteir, Ann B., 1941–   .

HQ1180.G72 1996   305.4'071'1   C96-932243-7

Contents

Struggling with Questions

Praxis

Preface

Essays in this book arose from an international conference held at York University in May 1995. Faculty, students, and programme administrators came from across Canada and the United States, and from universities in England and South Africa, eager to participate in formal discussion and informal exchange about graduate education in Women's Studies.

Organized by York's Graduate Programme in Women's Studies, the conference, "Graduate Women's Studies: Visions and Realities," was funded by the Social Sciences and Humanities Research Council of Canada, and by a grant from the York Ad Hoc Research Fund. Conference sessions highlighted issues in curriculum development, models for programme development, and professional development for students, as well as questions about disciplinarity and interdisciplinarity. A plenary session focussed on global dimensions, and there was a workshop on action-oriented research.

At a time when Women's Studies faculty and academic colleagues are endeavouring to design innovative arenas for teaching and learning, the topic of graduate education in Women's Studies features on many institutional agendas. Essays in the section "Shaping Programmes" address a variety of models now in place for MA and PhD work in Women's Studies. They offer food for thought about the circumstances that produced the freestanding MA and PhD programme at York University, the collaborative model at the University of Toronto, the Boston-area consortium at Radcliffe College, and the joint MA in Women's Studies established and governed by three universities in Halifax. These essays chronicle notable successes and describe the strategies that brought them about. The essay about plans, still emergent, for a PhD in Women's Studies at the University of Iowa makes clear, however, that thoughtful proposals do not always prevail in the face of an inhospitable political climate.

Political issues external to our graduate programmes are matched by numerous in-house dilemmas. For all our efforts to found and entrench graduate programmes in Women's Studies, fundamental issues preoccupy us, and keep us talking and thinking. Essays in the section "Struggling with Questions" articulate on-going problems. Women's Studies, developing as a radical new area of knowledge, has challenged our understanding of discipline boundaries. But is it a new discipline in itself, or is its radical nature best understood as an interdisciplinary, multidisciplinary, or transdisciplinary lens? At the graduate level, should we seek legitimacy and standing by sculpting Women's Studies as an autonomous field, or should we, instead, anchor research and teaching in established disciplines and existing structures? These questions have conceptual, curricular, methodological, and pedagogical dimensions. The politics of knowledge formation also impinges on the world of academic writing; one essay in this section explores the complex internal encounter between patriarchy and how Women's Studies students write for the academy.

It is incontrovertible that, as graduate faculty, students, and programme administrators, we are creating a future in which, as essays in the final section demonstrate, Women's Studies is both theory and "praxis." But what forms should the application of Women's Studies ideas and ideals take? Students are already out in the field, teaching (and team-teaching) undergraduate courses in Women's Studies, pursuing professional development, and credentializing themselves for academic opportunities that are just over the horizon. An urgent question for some students and teachers concerns degrees of relationship between activism and the academy, between professionalizing post-graduate training and community involvement. What responsibilities do graduate programmes have to feminist activism? Should MA and PhD programmes in Women's Studies have a practicum component, or assist the women's movement by undertaking policy research for specific groups?

The title of this volume is an acknowledgement that graduate work in Women's Studies carries with it intellectual and political aspirations. Guided by visions, and yet cognizant of realities within university life in the 1990s, how do we then bring expectations to life and nourish the next generations of teachers and scholars of Women's Studies? Is there a danger of too much reality and too little vision? Many essays in this collection take note of metaphors, fables, and narratives that, shaping culture, shape our own sense of the work we are doing within graduate Women's Studies. Several discussions explore metaphors of home and homelessness to reflect on relations between Women's Studies, other disciplines, and the academy itself. Metaphors of community are pervasive, as are references to constructing feminist spaces in the university. I hope that the essays in this volume will contribute to on-going critical exchange about the field of graduate Women's Studies as we struggle to control our own narratives and shape our own history.

Ann B. Shteir
Director, Graduate Programme in Women's Studies
York University

Acknowledgements

Funding from the Social Sciences and Humanities Research Council of Canada made possible the publication of this volume; I wish to acknowledge the support shown by Hilda Nantais. Appreciation goes as well to Noli Swatman, Office of Research Administration, York University.

It is a great pleasure to acknowledge the work of Luciana Ricciutelli, Managing Editor, Inanna Publications and Education Inc., (operating as *Canadian Woman Studies/les cahiers de la femme*), in producing this book. Luciana Ricciutelli brought skill, dedication, and heart to the project.

The cover illustration, "Sapientia," is by Verna Linney, artist and PhD student in the Graduate Programme in Women's Studies, York University.

Shaping Programmes

Making the Vision a Reality

York University's Graduate Programme in Women's Studies

Ann B. (Rusty) Shteir
Graduate Programme in Women's Studies, York University

York University began offering freestanding MA and PhD degree work in Women's Studies in January of 1992. There is direct intake into our programme, and students receive the MA and the PhD in Women's Studies. Since welcoming the pioneering first five students four years ago, we have awarded 24 MA degrees; many of these were awarded as a "Magisteriate," a gender-neutral designation that York put in place in 1993, based on a research paper written by one of our MA students. We expect to award our first PhD—and the first PhD in Women's Studies in Canada—in 1997. This milestone belongs partly to the doctoral student, partly to us, and partly to the larger history of academic feminism.

York's Graduate Programme in Women's Studies already is a large programme, with nearly 70 students enrolled in part-time and full-time MA and PhD work. Students represent a wide age profile, as well as diverse backgrounds. Half that number are moving steadily toward the PhD, completing their coursework, preparing to write comprehensive exams, and forming the supervisory committees for their dissertations. They are entering into the rituals of professional development, presenting papers at conferences, and receiving assignments as teaching assistants in undergraduate courses in Women's Studies and related areas.

Programme requirements are organized around five core half-courses offered by the Graduate Programme in Women's Studies. Students are asked to take two core courses from among the following: Women and Culture, Women's

History, Feminist Methodology, Feminist Theory, and Women and Public Policy. Beyond that, in fulfillment of course requirements, students choose from among a small but growing number of elective Graduate Women's Studies courses, notably Identity and Voice: Women and Early Modern European Culture; Women, Ideology, and the State in Islamic Societies; and Women, Ethnicity, and Nationalism. Many courses also are cross-listed to us from other graduate programmes where they have been shaped by members of our programme faculty. Graduate Women's Studies has worked hard to create a vibrant programme culture for students and faculty. A required non-credit programme seminar series highlights the research of programme faculty, and also provides a forum for discussing issues in professional development for students. In 1992, a programme conference on Mary Wollstonecraft brought scholars together to reflect upon Wollstonecraft's life, ideas, and legacy. More recently, students were integral to planning the conference on "Graduate Women's Studies: Visions and Realities." They soon will be embarking on planning an international conference for graduate students in Women's Studies.

While the last few years have seen a flowering of graduate Women's Studies programmes in Canada, the U.S., and internationally, the garden is still small. Each case represents an attempt to nurture a feminist post-graduate training project within the local conditions of one's own institution. At York University, local circumstances as well as some strategic structural features have combined to enable us to build a graduate programme of strength and standing. Three institutional features were especially important in the historical development of York's Graduate Programme in Women's Studies:

(1) University support for interdisciplinary curricular innovation: York University was established during the late 1960s, and is, therefore, relatively unfettered by institutional traditions and entrenched disciplinary boundaries. The new university was shaped in deliberate contrast to the University of Toronto, something of the rich and established downtown Great Uncle or Aunt to the red-brick newcomers living on the outskirts. From the start, in addition to canonical departments of English, Economics, and History, York has had large undergraduate units in interdisciplinary Humanities and Social Science, whose courses were a mandated part of undergraduate curricular requirements. The earliest undergraduate Women's Studies courses were offered under the already institutionalized rubrics of Humanities and Social Science.

Interdisciplinary graduate-level programmes came out of this same climate.

For some years, feminist graduate work found a niche through the Interdisciplinary MA Programme and the Graduate Programme in Social and Political Thought. Additionally, the Graduate Programme in English harboured a stream called "Women's Studies in Literature."

(2) A critical mass of feminist faculty: During the early 1970s, the new university made many hirings. It was a happy coming together of demography and feminist history, for that was the time in North America when young women of my generation were finishing their PhDs and also still going to consciousness-raising groups. Women who were newly hired by York University, and often in interdisciplinary programmes, flexed feminist muscles, and contributed to fresh directions in curriculum and teaching. Over the years, these faculty members attained significant academic and institutional standing; some shaped undergraduate degree programmes in Women's Studies. The initiative for a graduate programme came, in part, from those curricular pioneers who were doing the innovative work for which they were hired. By the time plans developed for the Graduate Programme in Women's Studies, a number of central players were already senior Associate Professors and Full Professors. They therefore could shepherd proposals through committees with considerable presence and clout.

(3) A broad university climate for Women's Studies/feminist initiatives: The proposal for the Graduate Programme in Women's Studies emerged in tandem with a proposal for the Centre for Feminist Research, York's organization for initiating and promoting feminist activities and collaborative research. Both in turn arose within a context of feminist presences on campus that include a Women's Studies library, an active Status of Women office, and a Women's Centre. These multiple presences have been strategically important in naturalizing feminist voices and ideas at York.

The Graduate Programme in Women's Studies is, therefore, an outgrowth of other academic work at York, situated in a context of curricular and institutional innovation.

The first two years in the life of this programme had the rosy glow of achievement, promise, and celebratory self-congratulation. We shaped new structures, and treasured each student who chose to join our journey. But, not surprisingly, complaints surfaced quickly from students who wanted all the wrinkles ironed out yesterday. Urgent questions emerged, and continue to emerge, that have made us put self-congratulation aside and hunker down to the work of putting vision into academic, curricular, and administrative practice.

We have been preoccupied by issues about field definition and discipline formation in Women's Studies. Is Women's Studies a lens, a perspective upon scholarship? Or, is Women's Studies a discipline unto itself, with its own methods and holy books? Some of our group take the position that all feminist approaches to scholarship belong in a Women's Studies graduate programme. Others hold the view that all Women's Studies is feminist scholarship, but not all feminist approaches to scholarship are "Women's Studies." Such matters surface in the work of the Admissions Committee when considering why an applicant wants to pursue academic interests in an interdisciplinary Women's Studies programme, rather than in a discipline such as History or Sociology. The same consideration enters into committee discussion about proposed dissertation and thesis topics. Most work in our programme is, in fact, feminist work that focusses on women rather than on gender theory without fairly specific reference to women.

Our discussions about the reading list for the PhD comprehensive examination are pertinent here. After completing doctoral coursework, students are required to write two exams: a general field exam, and an exam in a chosen area of specialization that will link to their dissertation. We now have two models in place for these exams. In option #1, students are examined on texts selected from a general field reading list established by the programme. The general field list under this model assumes ideas about "core" readings, while also allowing for a principle of substitution. (Students establish their own specialization list.) In option #2, students work with their individual comprehensive examination committee, to establish a list of books and articles in some stipulated areas, and identify central issues and questions on which to be examined in the general field exam. (Students establish their own specialization list.) This second option was developed by a joint student-faculty group made up principally of colleagues working in the social sciences and feminist theory. Opposing text-based approaches, they challenged the idea of core readings as well as the notion that we can know what Women's Studies is. Instead, they favoured an issue-centered approach tailored to the problematics and individualized interests of students.

Models for the PhD comprehensive examination in Women's Studies have been a vexed topic within our programme, but have been the basis for invigorating and fruitful debate. We currently are reflecting upon comprehensives from the vantage of students and faculty members who have participated in the examination process. As Programme Director, sitting ex officio on all comprehensive exam committees, I am concerned that students who choose option #2, in which they shape their own lists and questions, may not be stretching across the field of Women's Studies broadly enough. Instead of stepping into challenging new configurations, they may be clustering in familiar disciplinary areas. There is a tendency, for example, to stay at home in theory and the social sciences, rather than to cultivate historical perspectives. What might we do to ensure greater intellectual spread by means of course-work and through parameters set on comprehensive exams?

I am also concerned that students are reading such widely disparate materials in preparation for exams under option #2 that they have few common texts about which to talk with one another. Instead of commonalities among our doctoral students, there appears to be fragmentation. How can we ensure that students engage with both the humanities and the social sciences, and also draw on other areas as they learn to produce new knowledge in Women's Studies? Are there some books and articles that we believe everyone would do well to know about by the time they finish their degrees? These questions face off against fears of canonicity and misgivings about discipline formation.

Such matters fold back into discussion about core courses in several ways. Initially, the proposed curriculum for the Graduate Programme in Women's Studies included one core course that would serve as a meeting ground and start point for all incoming students. The plan foundered quickly on the shoals of disagreement about which texts and what issues to feature in the course. The devolution into courses across a range of areas followed.

Now, questions of audience and intellectual thresholds for the core course(s) have become more pressing as increasing numbers of students enter from undergraduate majors in Women's Studies. Graduate work in Women's Studies must assume that it builds upon prior undergraduate (or equivalent) familiarity with issues, vocabulary, and texts. Yet the reality is that students have many entry points into advanced feminist study. A student coming from the social sciences may be steeped in theory and methodology, but have had little contact with culture and history, and humanists versed in feminist literary theory may not have explored issues about public policy. How can we make core courses for the MA and PhD resonate most effectively? Should the core courses offer students opportunities to step more deeply into areas where they are already at home intellectually, or should core courses function as a form of distribution requirement, giving students language and perspectives outside their areas of familiarity? (Underlying any discussion about core courses is the question of what topic areas should be designated as core. Our programme offerings are, to date, meagre in the areas of global feminisms, science, sexualities, and religion. Are those areas equally important, equally core, for post-graduate knowledge production in Women's Studies?)

We in (graduate) Women's Studies are shaping a new contestatory discipline, and we should not be impeded by all-too-easy charges of canonicity. Women's Studies is, as I see it, an epistemologically astute interdisciplinary discipline. *C'est tout.* By now, there surely are feminist "classics" in our field, books and essays that have shaped some questions that we ask, or that have given us analytic tools and vocabulary. Graduate Women's Studies programmes should be acquainting students with these texts, with foundational issues and questions. Why are we so afraid of discipline formation in Women's Studies?

While questions about field definition in Women's Studies preoccupy us, we also ask where the jobs will be for our graduate students. A question for them, and also for us, it involves ideals as well as pragmatics. The York experience thus far suggests that pragmatics take no set form. Some students who began with a discipline-based degree come to York for a Women's Studies MA, and then return to a discipline-based PhD. Others who began in a discipline at the BA level move into Women's Studies for an MA and find themselves fully at home in Women's Studies. For some students, their sense of intellectual comfort calls for a footing in traditional disciplines; job prospects in the region where they want to live may also shape the direction of their degree work. For degree work in Women's Studies is about credentializing themselves for teaching in Women's Studies programmes. For others still, it validates their sense of self, or gives the opportunity to contribute to a feminist future by means of their research and writing.[1]

One of our responsibilities in graduate programmes in Women's Studies is to help students succeed in their chosen directions while also acknowledging practicalities. At York it means encouraging students to shape their graduate work as a kind of portfolio: showing some spread in the topics on which they write, being strategic in selecting texts and areas for the comprehensive examination; establishing a dissertation topic and dissertation committee with an eye to the kind of work students want their degree to guide them towards. I also think that we have the political responsibility to work toward hiring students with graduate degrees in Women's Studies. If we do not think ahead to the job advertisements and to membership on Hiring Committees, who will?

I have been reflecting upon the state of the field of graduate Women's Studies in a university where we have official status and considerable institutional support. More than just tolerated, we bring in much-valued student enrollment. And we are valued as "cutting edge" in a university that parades pioneers. The York MA and PhD programme offers some real structural indicators of progress in the field of Women's Studies as our students win prestigious scholarships and are invited to give public lectures. Faculty from a broad range of areas seek affiliation with us, shape new courses, and work with students. (The programme faculty consists of nearly 60 colleagues from across the humanities and social sciences, from Osgoode Hall Law School, and from the Faculties of Education, Environmental Studies, and Fine Arts.)

My confidence about our new field of knowledge is a bright flame in a gloomy climate as we and our students breathe the downsized air of contemporary Ontario and university life. In a climate of economic restructuring, I worry about funding for students as fees rise. I worry about the teaching and supervisory workload for graduate faculty as class sizes increase at the undergraduate level. I worry about research funding support for faculty members who propose Women's Studies topics to external agencies that do not have the category of "Women's Studies," and are seeing their own budgets slashed. The woman-friendly university is not yet at hand, and tough economic times often witness reassertions of patriarchal forms.

Recently, I participated in a research workshop at the Humboldt University in Berlin on "Curricular Transformation through Women's Studies/Gender Studies in Germany and Canada." The German university structure mitigates against the development of an autonomous Women's Studies curriculum; hierarchical, and shaped as fiefdoms, universities in both parts of a reunified Germany afford limited institutional space for curricular innovation. Colleagues there who seek to move beyond the template of "feminist topics in literature" are using the language not of "Women's Studies" but rather of "Gender Studies." Why, we asked, have they made that choice? We explained to them that nowadays in North America "Gender Studies" can be read, variously, as particularly progressive, or as conservative and "post-feminist." For our German colleagues, it seems that "Gender Studies" links to the social sciences, and is thus considered more "scientific" than "Women's Studies" (which they equate with culture and the humanities). "Gender Studies" also plays as more inclusive and less political than "Women's Studies."

Such features in contemporary German feminist academic culture serve to remind me that terminology and strategies for institutionalization and for resistance arise out of local circumstances, and that choices we make about graduate Women's Studies are situated within divergent regional, historical, and political climates. We have much work still to do in shaping graduate programmes in Women's Studies for the future. I want to end not with pragmatics but, instead, by reasserting some of what keeps us going as teachers and students: re-vision, reconfiguration, and cultivating and disseminating new knowledge for purposes of personal and social transformation.

Footnotes

[1]We should be asking students to reflect publicly on what brings them to MA/PhD work in Women's Studies. What kinds of meaning does graduate work in Women's Studies have for them? Has anyone begun to formulate such a study and chronicle responses?

Collaborating on Women's Studies

The University of Toronto Model

Kay Armatage
Cinema Studies and Women's Studies, University of Toronto

In 1994-95 the University of Toronto Graduate Collaborative Programme in Women's Studies completed its first year of operation, offering graduate degrees at all levels in the humanities, social sciences, and life sciences. As of August 1996 we have 50 students enrolled in 18 departments, including French, Religious Studies, Social Work, Law, and Community Health.

Structure

Graduate studies at the University of Toronto comprise a range of institutional models, including graduate departments, research centres, and institutes. A recent addition to the institutional structure is the collaborative programme, which brings together existing courses and faculty across cognate units (e.g., Ancient Studies, comprised of the graduate departments of Classical Studies, History of Art, and Near Eastern Studies). Students enroll in one of the collaborating departments but can access courses and faculty across units for specialization within the field. The academic potential of such a structure includes extensive cross-fertilization among departments, multi- and interdisciplinarity, specialization within a field, renewal of research fields through the innovative incorporation of disparate models and methodologies, and the new communities of scholars and potentials for joint research which can emerge from such novel groupings.

In many ways, the collaborative structure seems made for Women's Studies, as it continues at the graduate level a pattern common to many undergraduate programmes. The University of Toronto undergraduate Women's Studies Programme is not unique in gathering together cross-listed courses from disparate deparments, encouraging interdisciplinarity within degrees as well as within courses, and dispersing Women's Studies methodologies and research topics across a broad range of traditional disciplines. For the student at the graduate level, there are significant benefits to be gained from the collaborative degree, notably the potentially advantageous academic capital of a dual degree which includes qualification in an established discipline as well as certification in the interdisciplinary specialization of Women's Studies. There is another benefit which has already been relayed to us anecdotally again and again: often isolated as the lone feminist student in the department and alienated from the prevailing tendencies in their discipline, students in the Graduate Women's Studies Programme find themselves in a community of scholars with whom their research finally can be shared and their interests embraced.

The institutional advantage of such a model is readily apparent: a collaborative programme tends to cost next to nothing and reaps high returns. A collaborative programme usually consists of a small number of collaborating units. Using existing faculty and courses, it involves no direct appointments. Since the chair is usually also the chair of one of the collaborating units, the necessary infrastructure is already in place. The School of Graduate Studies' notion is that a collaborative programme will need a portion of a secretary's time, a few dollars for a brochure, and a drawer in a filing cabinet for storing records.

After nearly ten years of heroic work by Professor Kathryn Morgan (Philosophy and Women's Studies)—consulting, lobbying, planning, writing reports and proposals (the earliest dated 1985)—Women's Studies was convinced to opt for the collaborative model, initially for the simple reason that it could be done.

In an increasingly straitened academic economy, the prospects of mounting a new unit requiring infrastructure, faculty, and resources, as one might expect of a freestanding graduate degree programme, seemed like a dim light flickering on a distant horizon. A collaborative programme, on the other hand, could be mounted now.

Despite the joyful satisfaction of seeing a decade's labours and hopes come to fruition, there were some justified fears about adopting such a model. The undergraduate programme at the University of Toronto is severely under-resourced and has been since its inception 25 years ago. With 2.43 Full Time Equivalents (FTEs) appointed to the core faculty (an increase of only .69 FTEs over ten years), only two of the six core faculty hold the majority of their appointment in Women's Studies. Thus, most of the faculty have their principal obligations in other departments, requiring double participation on departmental and college committees and at social and intellectual events. Some of the Women's Studies core courses are still taught on a stipendiary basis. Therefore, staffing and curriculum stability remain primary issues. As a result of the paucity of resources at the undergraduate level, Women's Studies faculty feared that the graduate programme would be a double drain, both on the undergraduate programme and on their own scholarship.

A second concern was the economy of a collaborative model, specifically the assumption that additional resources would not be necessary. New College (the college "home" of the undergraduate programme) is mandated as an undergraduate unit supporting college programmes (not departments, either undergraduate or graduate) and therefore the graduate programme could not expect administrative support from an undergraduate college. Thus no administrative infrastructure was readily available in the existing Women's Studies undergraduate programme or its college base.

Another expected source of infrastructure, supplies, equipment, facilities, and institutional base for a collaborative programme is normally the collaborating units themselves. Since a collaborative programme draws together faculty and courses already in existence, the collaborating units are expected to be the principal source of support for the programme, and the programme directorship, administrative support, office, and the like are expected to rotate among the chairs of the collaborating departments. In the case of Women's Studies at the University of Toronto, however, this was an extremely unlikely scenario, since none of the existing chairs of the collaborating units were linked to Women's Studies either through institutional affiliations or research interests. And although there was tremendous support from the collaborating departments in terms of faculty participation and course offerings, the partnering units were less enthusiastic about simply handing over a portion of their own budgets to form a funding base for the new graduate programme.

The resolution of the resource question came about through a combination of strategy and happenstance. The lack of direct support from the collaborating units worked strategically in our favour, for it pointed to the need for base funding, a new wrinkle on the collaborative model. The material requirements of the new graduate programme were further underlined by my appointment as programme director.

I am something of an anomaly at the University of Toronto. Cross-appointed to Cinema Studies (.66) and Women's Studies (.33), both undergraduate college programmes, I have no departmental affiliation. My appointment to the School of Graduate Studies is through the Graduate Centre for the Study of Drama (not a department either). Such byzantine institutional complications in fact proved to be advantageous to the graduate programme, principally because my appointment brought with it no infrastructure whatsoever. Addi-tional resources were thus seen to be necessary to the establishment of the Graduate Women's Studies Programme. Due to the support of the President, the Provost, and the School of Graduate Studies, a budget was allocated to the graduate programme not only for infrastructure (administrative assistant, equipment, furniture) and to "buy out" my obligations to the undergraduate programme, but also for the programme launch (advertising, brochure, events). Thus the Graduate Collaborative Programme in Women's Studies was founded with unprecedented support.

The principal institutional advantage of the collaborative model, however, has been the exceptional intellectual commitment of the faculty to Women's Studies as a scholarly and pedagogical field. Women's Studies research and teaching already exist in abundance at the graduate level. With 18 collaborating units, we offer 112 graduate courses and over 90 faculty as potential teachers, supervisors, readers, and friendly advisors. Already the largest collaborative programme at the University of Toronto, it is apparent that we have only begun to tap the curricular and faculty resources in the field.

Another positive outcome emerges from the hierarchical intellectual politics of an institution whose mission is research excellence. As opposed to the undergraduate programme, which was "tainted" with its affiliations with the women's movement and had to fight repeated battles to establish its scholarly and pedagogical credibility, the graduate programme hit the ground with its head in the air. Because all of its faculty are already tenured and appointed to the School of Graduate Studies, many of them internationally known scholars, and, precisely because it is a collaborative (i.e., discipline-based) programme, the faculty are gilded with the purity of their disciplinary research. The institutional response is instant respect. Thelma McCormack has discussed the issue of legitimation as a continuing problem for Women's Studies (see article in this volume). The irony is that at the undergraduate level all but a few of the faculty are de-legitimized by their association with Women's Studies and its outreach-oriented commitment to a community-based women's movement, while the presence of the same women faculty at the graduate level becomes one of the legitimating factors of the collaborative programme.

Indeed, their participation in the graduate programme may now be the hoped for cash cow of the programme. As educational institutions increasingly see the necessity of breaking down the walls of the ivory tower (an understanding that Women's Studies at the undergraduate level was founded on), ties to the community outside the university will be the golden strings to the funding purses that post-secondary institutions will depend upon for the future.

There is a downside to this abundance. After one year in operation, it is pressingly evident that such a large programme requires extraordinary coordination. Despite the intellectual and curricular commitment, the collaborative programme is still an add-on for the administration of the collaborating units and for the time and energy of the faculty. Just to collect the annual course listings from 18 departments requires weeks of repeated phone calls, faxed reminders, and cajoling of graduate coordinators. Finding a meeting time for a programme committee of over 20 members (including student representatives) is an organizational nightmare, while getting already over-committed faculty to participate in fund-raising projects, extra committees, and social/intellectual events is virtually impossible.

Women's Studies, the Disciplines, and Interdisciplinarity

The burning question of the day with Women's Studies is the value of the graduate degrees. This brings us to the question of the collaborative model from the point of view of the students.

We have already heard via Women's Studies meetings, electronic conferences and bulletin boards on the internet, and student word of mouth, that feelings of "homelessness" persist in freestanding Women's Studies graduate programmes. Some students who have specialized in Women's Studies at the undergraduate level have no disciplinary base except Women's Studies, and among both faculty and students there still remains little consensus as to what exactly constitutes the field. In a collaborative graduate programme, on the other hand, the traditional disciplines provide the point of entry to an interdisciplinary programme. To enter the Graduate Collaborative Programme at the University of Toronto, students have to be admitted through one of the collaborating units, and they will exit the programme with a disciplinary degree buttressed by a "notation" of their specialization in Women's Studies.

Because students enter the programme through a traditional department, a base of disciplinary canonical knowledge and research methodology can be assumed. Still the questions remain: are they qualified to do Women's Studies at the graduate level and what does that mean? We regularly receive eager inquiries about the programme from would-be applicants who list volunteer work in feminist organizations as Women's Studies credentials, apparently unaware of the specific taxonomy of Women's Studies as an academic discourse. In our admissions meetings, we try to be flexible about our definitions of "suitable background in Women's Studies," but nevertheless we express in our admission and degree requirements a commitment to Women's Studies as an advanced field of research and scholarship bringing interdisciplinarity into the disciplines.

Women's Studies as a field has been characterized by interdisciplinarity, combining and crossing disciplines in scholarship, pedagogy, and theory. Also because the Collaborative Programme comprises faculty, courses, and departments from three divisions of the graduate school, the potential for multi-disciplinarity is fundamental to its institutional structure. Theoretically, a student in history, for example, could support work in that discipline with relevant courses in law or medicine, crossing the boundaries of the divisions of humanities, social sciences, and life sciences.

The potential for multi-disciplinarity in our programme is, however, more apparent than real. Students in the Collaborative Programme in Women's Studies have to fulfill all the degree requirements of their home departments as well as the requirements of our programme. Although there are no strict limits to the number of courses that can be taken in a degree, an outside minor will tend to consist solely of the Women's Studies requirements, rather than the freewheeling canter across the open range of graduate divisions that at first seemed possible.

For some feminist scholars, multi-disciplinarity is not an issue, as Women's Studies is asserted as an (interdisciplinary) discipline in its own right with a specific body of knowledge to be mastered. Others worry that the attempt to establish canonicity will degenerate into the patriarchal fortress that we find in the established disciplines. For scholars in many fields, the push to define new areas of research and scholarship as disciplines is not only institutionally but academically retrogressive. Prominent scholars in Cinema Studies, for example, see that field as choking itself to death; its foremost scholars are fleeing to multi- and cross-disciplinary research, leaving the most conservative hanging onto Cinema Studies as a "discipline," the last of the high arts, carving out a self-immolating position of effete and unmarketable specialization. The transformative, self-critical nature of Women's Studies, combined with the emphasis on postcolonial and poststructural approaches which ceaselessly question the established canons and canonicity itself, is seen as the check against such retrograde tendencies.

A similar argument has been applied to another aspect of the University of Toronto model, the required core course. Our core course addresses the range of scholarly and theoretical approaches to Women's Studies: feminist pedagogy, canonicity, methodological specificity, the intricacies of feminist research, and differences between conceptions of Women's Studies, feminist studies, and gender studies. That such a course is retrograde is argued on two bases, theory and praxis. The theoretical objection is that the core curriculum model articulates Women's Studies as a discipline with specific bodies of knowledge or approaches to knowledge; this flies in the face of current intellectual movements which emphasize multi- and interdisciplinarity. The praxis argument is self-evident: as the four-year full-fee PhD gallops towards us, time and money are increasingly pressing factors. Additional degree requirements are seen to be a deterrent to advanced work in the field, outweighing the potential market advantage of a degree with dual credentials.

Happily, our experience thus far repudiates this second argument. Our students are delighted to participate in the core course. For students in large, male-dominated departments, the required Women's Studies core course is often the only course in their graduate career in which they are able to find a sympathetic feminist faculty member, encounter other students working in the field, and speak freely about their concerns as women in their home discipline. Students enrolled this year in the coordinated research seminar, a course required only of PhD students, have seen the opportunity for cross-disciplinary exchange at an advanced level as one of the intellectual advantages of participation in the programme, enriching not only their sense of scholarly community but their own research as well.

Spanners in the Works

There are four remaining problems, one academic, one financial, one structural/institutional, and the fourth one touching on economics, politics, philosophy.

The first problem is that despite the widely acknowledged strengths of the University of Toronto undergraduate Women's Studies Programme, there is no avenue for entry by Women's Studies specialists to the graduate programme. If graduands have completed a twenty-course degree with a ten-course specialization in Women's Studies, they are unlikely to have the additional necessary disciplinary qualifications for admission to one of the collaborating departments. Our most highly qualified students must go elsewhere for graduate degrees in their area of specialization.

We are already encountering at least two different outcomes of the lack of interface between the graduate and undergraduate programmes. One predictable outcome is a receding enrolment in the specialist degree. Since a double major in Women's Studies and a traditional discipline provides suitable qualification for entry to the collaborative programme—indeed provides the only ramp to the University of Toronto programme—the senior seminars, which traditionally offer the most satisfying forays into the field for both faculty and students, may begin to languish for customers. Those few who pursue the more advanced scholarship available at the senior undergraduate level become the most highly qualified students (our best among them) who must seek graduate work elsewhere.

Another—ever-present—problem is funding. As admission to the graduate school is controlled by departments, Women's Studies students are at the mercy of departmental funding priorities for Ontario Graduate Fellowships and teaching assistantships. The best Women's Studies students may well find themselves on the lower rungs of the disciplinary funding paradigm. As a new programme, moreover, we have no alumnae base, no endowments which might finance independent entrance scholarships for Women's Studies.

The third is lack of structural/institutional synergy. Although the institutional structure of a large university like the University of Toronto is particularly byzantine, I suspect that the historical development and the present configuration of Women's Studies are not unique to us. Women's Studies has grown apace in 25 years, and is now scattered across undergraduate and graduate units in the humanities, social sciences, and life sciences on the St. George and satellite college campuses; faculty, programmes, and research resources are separately funded, administered, and housed. Such dissemination appears at first blush as a sign of institutional support as well as of the quality and quantity of student interest, faculty expertise, and resource riches. At the same time, it signals lack of synergy and promotes isolation, frustration, and waste for students, faculty, and administration alike. The duplication of infrastructures for the graduate and undergraduate programmes on the St. George campus alone is a case in point. Another is the separation of research resources. Scholars must trek to a number of different locations and master different indexing systems to access the total Women's Studies research offerings at the University of Toronto. With no central administrative umbrella, communication among units has been notoriously haphazard, requiring incessant administrative vigilance to track course offerings, curricular overlap, activities, events, resources (how many separate mailing lists can there be in one institution?). The ideal of a community of interested scholars remains a distant dream even within one institution.

Finally, there are the particular political/economic contours of the contemporary conjuncture, leading to pressing philosophical questions such as the ones outlined by Mary Evans in "Whose Direction? Whose Mainstream? Women's Studies and the Politics of the Contemporary University" (see article in this volume). Although the pressures of the market have brought about the democratization of education and concomitant benefits for women and Women's Studies, Evans cautions against embracing such apparently positive changes too hastily. Predominant economic interests erode definitions of success with the values and standards of the market. Students as consumers, the creation of internal markets which align with perceived need, the pressures of enrolment, the marketability of degrees, and the movement of exclusion/ elitism in specific centres have significant effects on women in the academy. The paradox of the latter is already apparent at the University of Toronto, as the Graduate Women's Studies Programme is founded just at the moment when the casualized (stipendiary) teaching at the centre of the undergraduate programme is most threatened by government cutbacks to post-secondary education. As the School of Graduate Studies is struggling to survive as a unit, the Graduate Collaborative Programme in Women's Studies appears as a potential golden girl: high student interest and ties to the community outside the university bring the hope of new funding sources.

Conclusion

The future of graduate Women's Studies rests on the transformation of these problems into solutions. As Mary Evans asserts, present conditions require feminist scholars to maintain a primary interest in the narrative of knowledge. Rather than seeing ourselves as separate, subversive, gnawing away at the entrails of the disciplines, we must maintain our control and centrality. In addition to maintaining theoretical control of the category "women," our potential as golden girl can be realized precisely as a centring.

At present, Women's Studies at the University is in the midst of a Provostial Review. A prestigious committee has been gathered at the highest level of academic administration with a mandate to examine institution-wide administrative structures, resources, and facilities as well as to vet academic reviews of the St. George campus undergraduate and graduate programmes. Although the committee's task is enormous, we are cautiously optimistic about its outcome.

While realizing full well the resistance to initiatives which appear to create new units, we believe equally in the value of our Women's Studies Programmes and the available institutional support for excellence. The transformation of our problems into solutions can be achieved literally at the University of Toronto with the creation of a central administrative umbrella which combines graduate and undergraduate units, a collaborative graduate programme with a freestanding degree and graduate research centres. A centre for Women's Studies and feminist research could gather together the disparate Women's Studies units and resources, providing an admissions ramp for undergraduate specialists into the graduate programme. While effecting the desired synergy of rationalized resources, a centre could also create the community of interested scholars who can work together for the production of a sane human future.

Inventing a Feminist Institution
An Informal History of the Graduate Consortium in Women's Studies at Radcliffe

Ruth Perry
Literature Faculty, Massachusetts Institute of Technology

For three years now, the Graduate Consortium in Women's Studies at Radcliffe College has been offering experimental courses taught by faculty from more than one institution in the Boston area, trained in at least two different disciplines, to graduate students in a variety of fields from the contributing institutions. In 1993-4 we offered these subjects: Feminist Methodologies taught by an historian, a sociologist, and a literary critic; Boundaries of Domesticity in Early Modern Europe taught by an art historian, a literary critic, and a European historian, considering how an ideal of the "domestic" arose in the early modern period, what it stood for and what it opposed; Sexuality, and Culture in the U.S. and Latin America, taught by an anthropologist and a literary comparatist, examining the construction, deconstruction, and resistance of sexual subjects in the U.S. and Latin America; and Narratives of Kinship in Periods of Emerging Capitalism, taught by a literary critic and an anthropologist, looking at the effects on women of industrialization including the narrativization of experience and the impact of print culture.

How the Grad Con (as we familiarly call it) was conceived and established, what snags we ran into, what worked and what did not, is a very long story.

This project began as a conversation among friends in 1988. Six white women in their forties and fifties who taught in Boston-area universities, we were trained in traditional disciplines, connected to Women's Studies since the 1970s, and politically left of center. We dreamed up the Consortium

21

because we wanted to work together in an institution of our own. That the impetus came from faculty rather than from administrators or even students shaped much of what followed.

For one thing, we wanted to retrieve the thrilling interdisciplinarity that operated in the old days when there were only five feminists on any campus and we talked across disciplines because all we had was each other. Those '70s explorations led to useful generalizations about the socialization of men and women, about the construction of what was natural, about the division of labour by class and gender, about how context affected all ideas, and about the erasure of bodily knowledge from academic learning. By now, of course, new feminist questions have arisen in the political and economic context of the '90s—questions about mobile capital and immobile women, about media monopolies and gender-bending—questions that no single discipline can handle. But Women Studies' limited success in the academy has made feminist scholars more acceptable to their departments, where they burrow ever-deeper into their own disciplines. Moreover, disciplines themselves have become more and more specialized as the job market tightens. Needless to say, we were also concerned about training the next generation of feminist scholars.

Boston, like many metropolitan areas in the United States, boasts a great many academic institutions in geographically close proximity. Yet there is little and only very selective contact among students and faculty from different institutions. Most feminist scholars in these institutions feel like "token" members of their own departments and/or institutions; the same is true of graduate students interested in feminist scholarship. But together feminists in this metropolitan area constitute an intellectual community with great diversity, range, and power.

The original idea behind the Consortium was to regroup these "token" faculty feminists from Boston's institutions of higher learning for their own intellectual advancement and psychic restitution, and for graduate student training—to explore ideas generated by an analysis of race, ethnicity, class, and gender as played out in our postcolonial, postmodern, and multicultural world. This would be an institution where we could teach on the borders of academic disciplines where our research interests came together, and create interdisciplinary and cross-cultural approaches to new topics that existed nowhere else in traditional curricula. We wanted to put our pedagogical skills where our hearts were, so to speak, and to bring to one enterprise the feminist intellectual labor that remained alienated and fragmented in our separate home institutions.

The initial "what if" conversations among friends soon widened to include a working group of interested colleagues from several other schools in the Boston area: Brandeis University, Boston College, Harvard University (its Graduate School of Arts and Sciences, Divinity School, and Graduate School of Education), Massachusetts Institute of Technology, Northeastern and Tufts Universities.

The earliest meetings were informal gatherings over a bottle of wine in my kitchen. Friendship was crucial to the mix. None of us would have taken on the Grad Con if seeing one another had not been an added bonus. The Consortium meetings were a welcomed opportunity to get together; even the endless round-robin phone calling to set a time when everyone could meet had its pleasures. Our affection for one another rewarded our efforts and replenished our energy.

At these kitchen meetings we discussed such beginning ideas as: What is a Consortium and how should it work? Who should be included in the membership? What kinds of courses should be offered? How should the Consortium be governed? Where should it be based? Where could we locate support? These questions involved many different intellectual, political, and management issues and it was heartening how the relevant skill and knowledge to address them kept surfacing among us, moving the ideas along.

We worked out the Consortial model: courses would be taught by inter-disciplinary teams involving faculty from at least two institutions for the benefit of graduate students from any of the contributing institutions. The idea was to invent unique courses in areas of contemporary academic concern that could not be taught in any single department or at any single university, but that drew on the faculty resources of several. Courses would be for enrichment rather than matriculation, and would supplement rather than replace existing graduate sequences.

Our intellectual criteria were fairly simple. Courses would have to be: (1) interdisciplinary, that is, team-taught by faculty members trained in at least two different disciplines and including both approaches in every class; (2) innovative, that is, committed to breaking new ground and developing new materials rather than reviewing, summarizing, or presenting the latest research; (3) epistemologically self-conscious, that is, explicitly aware of the historical and cultural location of the intellectual sources on which they drew. Even courses dealing with purely theoretical approaches would be expected to put into historical and cross-cultural perspective the sources of the theories they examined and developed.

The only other inviolate principle we articulated early on was the processual principle of governance by a rotating, collective body drawn from participating institutions. We were convinced then, as we are now, that this one overriding principle would ensure the democratic flexibility of the institution to serve a variety of different purposes and prevent any one group or individual from dominating it. We felt that if intellectual and policy decisions were made by such a rotating, collective group, we could trust the process to take care of whatever issues came up.

By the time Radcliffe came into the picture in 1990, we had agreed on another administrative principle: teaching our seminars would be counted in the regular workload of faculty members, rather than being done as an overload, a second job, as was too often true of women's—and Women's Studies—work. For this reason we needed funding to replace a faculty member absent from one course at her home institution when that person was teaching a Consortium course. Radcliffe provided the essential funding for release time and an infrastructure for arranging course credit, both crucial contributions to this experiment in higher education.

Our rotating governing body took shape by 1991. All intellectual decisions (as opposed to administrative decisions) were to be made by an advisory group of representatives drawn from the Women's Studies programmes at each institution. That is, the Women's Studies programmes at each school, rather than deans or department heads, chose the representative from each institution. We sent out the call through the Women's Studies programmes of the participating institutions, inviting faculty and graduate students to discuss the courses they would like to teach and to take. We needed to identify potential faculty to teach, as well as the subject areas that graduate students thought needed collaborative and interdisciplinary work. At this point we saw how the limitations in standard recruitment practice would also limit us. For example, we found that economists with an interest in gender, or scientists interested in feminist questions—or even psychologists working on gender—were in short supply in Boston. Situating our initiative within existing institutions meant living with—and trying to remedy—the effects of structures and values already in place in those institutions: hierarchical power, competition, idealization of the individual scholar working alone, as well as the racism, elitism, and sexism that operated in the selection of faculty and students.

We also soon realized that although the idea of interdisciplinary work was generally admired, scholars did not actually *know* the cutting edge work—or even the particular people doing it—outside of their own fields. Feminist scholars largely tended to know others in their generic fields (e.g., literature, history, sociology) in neighbouring institutions, but not feminists working in other disciplines at other universities. So we developed a strategy for "intellectual matchmaking" for purposes of course development, sending out blanket invitations for Saturday morning networking sessions to all Women's Studies faculty at the participating institutions. Over coffee and muffins we would describe the Consortium, explain its potential, and then ask everyone present to introduce themselves and their work to the others. Each person in the circle would tell what s/he was working on, what kind of course s/he would like to teach, and what kind of intellectual collaboration s/he was looking for. These brainstorming sessions came closer than any other activity to embodying the Consortium's original goal—to create a new institution in which bureaucratic forms gave way to feminist intellectual consciousness-raising, and in which collaborative work created a feminist community across institutional boundaries. These meetings provided faculty an opportunity to meet colleagues from other disciplines and other institutions. They demonstrated how the Consortium could be a resource for feminist intellectuals and a wellspring for intellectual innovation. Interestingly, most of the courses generated to date have been taught by faculty who met in the midst of great enthusiasm at one of our networking sessions.

We also organized more focused seminars on particular subject areas that we thought needed attention, inviting all potential Consortium faculty with interests in the topics. These were more like mini-conferences, lasting a morning or an afternoon, and were facilitated by Board members and several invited local experts on the topic under discussion.

Meanwhile our campus representatives were working with the appropriate dean or committee on each campus to explain the potential advantages of this arrangement for our home institutions and to allay residual doubts. We highlighted the fact that allowing graduate students to take Consortium courses without extra tuition charges would multiply the course offerings available at all schools and would make Boston institutions attractive to potential graduate students. The same was true of faculty: the Consortium would offer an attractive teaching possibility, thus giving these institutions an edge in faculty recruitment. The collaborative work in preparing and teaching interdisciplinary Consortium courses would provide genuine faculty development and enrichment in a formal work setting.

For graduate students as well, the chance to work with faculty from other Boston-area institutions would increase their range of professional connections and simultaneously provide a wider community for students who were often isolated and unhappy at their individual institutions. Such arguments as these were attractive to many of the participating institutions' administrators.

Once we had an institutional structure, we made sure that the courses developed by potential faculty were indeed Consortium courses—that is, that they fit the original guidelines that the planning group had identified as essential to this new collaboration. Consortium courses were to be interdisciplinary, innovative, and epistemologically and culturally self-conscious; but we had no mechanism for insuring attention to these dimensions. We felt queasy about telling anyone what to teach; nobody ever really tells a faculty member what to do in the classroom, especially a senior faculty member. Because Consortium courses were supposed to allow faculty to teach their research interests, to help them break ground on new materials, all external directives seemed coercive and disrespectful. Still, we wanted to encourage certain kinds of explorations, such as placing questions of gender in a global context.

The process of actual course development proved unexpectedly delicate. No one was prepared for the touchiness of the teaching teams. In spite of hopes that we could contribute to one another's intellectual growth, improve one another's work, and constructively comment on syllabi, wounded feelings and defensiveness inevitably surfaced in the process of vetting courses and reviewing reading lists, a practice taken on by the Board of Directors from the very beginning. We realized too late how much rides on peer review in the academy to which we have been so well socialized. Jobs, tenure, raises, and publication (just to state a few of the stakes), with their inherent anxieties, all are granted or withheld on the basis of peer evaluation. It may be impossible to take criticism disinterestedly, we learned. When our first course review process caused wounded feelings among respected colleagues, we decided to arrange face-to-face meetings with the instructor teams rather than sending written suggestions. This made the process more collegial and dialogic, even if it did not end all potential for bruised pride. We learned that bringing bodies and minds together in one room is almost always preferable to, and likely to create more intellectual energy than, any form of long-distance communication.

Major differences about the meaning of "interdisciplinary" also surfaced surprisingly in the process of course planning, when we began to work through our definitions operationally. Feminist scholars in the Consortium who had been teaching and publishing in Women's Studies for some 20 years thought their work was already interdisciplinary. Many had worked on subjects that required knowledge of more than one field of study and multiple perspectives. But as the Board began to scrutinize proposed syllabi submitted for approval, and press for the *actual* collaboration of faculty teams in every single week's work a new and more advanced model of interdisciplinarity emerged.

What most of us had meant by interdisciplinary work until then involved bringing the information of several different academic disciplines to bear on a single problem. It was like training several spotlights, each a source of illumination, upon a single object. Each discipline's methods would discover different relevant truths about the object so that an "interdisciplinary approach" meant at least twice the analytic power of the merely uni-disciplinary approach. For example, to investigate the demise of small towns in the U.S., a historian might examine national economic trends in the context of international politics; a sociologist might detail the unraveling of the social fabric, the exodus of young people, the dwindling numbers of people in church; a fiction writer might describe—and a literary critic analyze—the symptoms, signs, aesthetics ,and affects of these changes: empty offices in town hall, abandoned warehouses, perennial going-out-of-business signs, stray cats on a dusty street. However, this form of interdisciplinarity leaves the methods of investigation in each discipline intact, integrating or synthesizing only at the level of findings. The historian, sociologist, and literary critic each describe their separate aspects of the problem—like the blind men describing the legs, sides, trunk, and tail of an elephant and then trying to describe a whole animal from each of these parts.

In contradistinction to this accepted model, the interdisciplinarity that evolved through the process of the Consortium Board meetings moved each interrogation much closer to the sources of our questions and the goals of our enterprise, asking what actually constitutes evidence or even insight when approaching a given problem—whether for the historian, the sociologist, or the literary critic. This turns out to be a much more difficult and radical sort of interdisciplinarity, in which the members of a team do not take turns presenting their discipline's take on a subject but slog through every aspect of the problem together, paying attention to their differences. Using this approach, the problem itself—the demise of small towns, for example—becomes only one of the foci, whereas the process of one discipline questioning the rhetoric, assumptions, and methods of another discipline becomes another set of foci. This is the point to which our insistence on the need for epistemological self-consciousness has led. To stay with the metaphor of the blind men describing the elephant, we began to try and encourage each investigator to be clear about which part of the elephant she was describing, what her evidence and methods were, and to pay attention to the evidence and methods of her co-investigators as well. Simply put, questions involving the forms of knowledge production became as important as the content of knowledge itself.

*****

Consortium courses have been fascinating to develop, to teach, and to take. Inevitably, in a course for graduate students with disparate academic backgrounds, taught by faculty trained in a variety of disciplines, confusions arise about the meanings of terms and the academic conventions of others' fields. We saw to our dismay that where the effort to translate between fields was kept rigorously alive by the teaching faculty, where disciplinary assumptions were continuously being interrogated, students, especially less advanced ones, were liable to get lost. Students have asked for less rather than more "feminist pedagogy." They want clarity, and coherent, measurable information; they want signposts attached to their tasks; they want to be told whither they are going and by what means and why. At least for some students, it is apparent that two of our original goals—interdisciplinarity and feminist decentralization of authority—are in tension with each other, at least in the classroom.

Finally, although we continue to cling to our chosen consensual process for making decisions, this has been, as anyone can tell you who has tried to run an organization non-hierarchically, an extremely time-consuming project. Board meetings take as much as three hours every three weeks. Board members and especially co-chairs confer with one another and with the coordinator in between: thinking, talking, drafting, editing memoranda to keep things going. All this is volunteer labor from feminist scholars already seriously overworked at their home institutions. But although most Board members walk into those late afternoon meetings exhausted from already packed days, we emerge paradoxically refreshed by our time together. This can only be because we talk about intellectual questions that really matter to us, trying to implement an idealistic vision of collective intellectual life.

A longer version of this article, with a fuller account of the process, has been published in the NWSA Journal *Summer 1996, 8 (2): 60-83.*

Creating Feminist Spaces in the University

Pat Baker
Sociology, Anthropology, and Women's Studies,
Mount Saint Vincent University,
Linda Christiansen-Ruffman
Sociology and Women's Studies, Saint Mary's University,
Ann Manicom
*Education and Women's Studies, Dalhousie University**

The notion of feminist space encompasses a variety of meanings: space as process, space as content, as well as space in the more literal sense of having a clearly delineated and distinct "home" for graduate Women's Studies in our universities. When we embarked on constructing a Joint Master of Arts in Women's Studies that would be jointly governed by three universities in Halifax—Mount Saint Vincent University, Dalhousie University, and Saint Mary's University[1]—each with different governing structures, we did not anticipate how long the process would take. After five years of planning and development, we are ready to start implementing the programme and have accepted our first students for the fall of 1996. The process of working collaboratively on a graduate programme has been a rich one. We hope that this essay conveys both the richness and the difficulties of the process.

Making Feminist Spaces

In general, we see Women's Studies programmes as having considerable potential to develop feminist spaces. Because of the vagaries of university institutions, those who are in isolated places—like Women's Studies programmes—can feel as though they are homeless and under attack. We, however, do not see ourselves collectively as "homeless," but rather as constructing a "home" base.

In creating our own spaces, we are trying to make the academy friendlier to women, more interdisciplinary, more equitable, more collaborative, and more engaged with the community and with social justice issues, both locally and globally. We do, however, recognize that this is an ongoing process and that the struggle is not over.

Background and Context

Unlike most other provinces in Canada, Nova Scotia historically has had a number of small universities, mainly undergraduate liberal arts colleges and universities, scattered around the region. They have produced a proud legacy of high quality education in the province, despite the somewhat peripheral and marginal socio-economic status of the Atlantic region within Canada. Federal funding has allowed us to maintain a quality post-secondary education system in the region, but these small, autonomous institutions lack a history of collaborative work. This was the context in which we were trying to develop collaboration among Women's Studies programmes at different universities.

During this period of time, especially in the early '70s and '80s, Mount Saint Vincent University was establishing itself as "the" women's university in Canada, a territorial boundary acceptable to the other local university administrations—not a boundary line they cared to fight. However, this territorial marker was unacceptable to women faculty members within the other universities who were trying to weave feminist ideas into their classes and who were interested in establishing Women's Studies majors in their own BA programmes. A number of events enabled feminist faculty at other universities to win the struggle for Women's Studies spaces at their own universities. This then provided a grounding for a joint Masters programme to develop.

Rooting Feminist University Spaces in Women's Movement Work

The joint MA in Women's Studies which began in September 1996 has been developing in a formal way since 1991.[2] But in many respects programme development has been a process for some 25 years. For most of us, our particular universities served as only one of our work spaces. Feminist faculty also had work spaces in the women's movement, and it was here, over a number of years, that the barriers began to be breached. Community and academic women came together in feminist movement activities and created feminist spaces outside the universities, although occasionally linked to university resources.

This involvement in feminist community activity made possible, over time, a history of collaboration among university faculty in the Halifax area—despite the institutional boundaries set in place by our respective places of employment.

Atlantic scholars have been very much at the forefront of the development of Women's Studies in Canada. In 1976 Halifax was the site of what became the first major national conference of research on women, a conference co-organized by women from the three major Halifax universities. That conference was the forerunner of the annual Canadian Research Institute for the Advancement of Women (CRIAW) conference. *Atlantis*, which has been called the first interdisciplinary Women's Studies journal in Canada, was created and continues to be located in this region. Further, it was an Atlantic Canadian initiative that prompted the Canadian government's Secretary of State to create five regional endowed Chairs of Women's Studies in Canada, one of which is the local Nancy Rowell Jackman Chair in Women's Studies, also known as Nancy's Chair in Women's Studies. Also, as of 1992, the Canadian government has designated Mount Saint Vincent University as the permanent location of a United Nations Focal Point for Women and Development.

Almost all faculty involved in these Women's Studies initiatives have also been active in the larger feminist community within Nova Scotia. The CRIAW-Nova Scotia co-ordinating group, for example, includes an equal number of members from the community and the university, and has representation from all three major universities. This has helped to weave trust among members from different campuses and disciplines.

In addition to connections forged in the '70s and '80s through community-based feminist work, faculty have been creating feminist spaces within their own universities through women's caucuses or associations. Both the Dalhousie Women's Faculty Organization and the Saint Mary's Women's Caucus have raised feminist issues on campus and within the larger community for over 20 years. Collaborative, inter-university work was fostered in 1983, when women representatives from each campus in Atlantic Canada participated in a week-long seminar on Women and Development with women faculty from the Caribbean, sponsored by the Association of Atlantic Universities. This seminar pointed to the need for better organization among women in Atlantic Canada and gave rise to the Atlantic Women and Development Committee (AWAND) which included membership from within and outside the academy. A number of collaborative ideas were discussed, including an Atlantic Canada based graduate programme in Women's Studies and CIDA projects.

In more recent years, local university faculty have a proven record of cooperative Women's Studies ventures among the universities. The Summer Institute on Gender and Development (SIGAD) was a joint programme of Women's Studies faculty at Saint Mary's and Dalhousie Universities; the Nigeria Linkage was a joint programme of Women's Studies faculty at Mount Saint Vincent and Dalhousie Universities; the Guyana Project was a Dalhousie project with membership on the Management Committee from Mount Saint Vincent and Saint Mary's Universities, representing AWAND.

This history of work in the women's movement and in our campus-based women's networks has helped to build trust and respect among us, and for each other's work. Nevertheless, it is no easy feat to convince universities who have not collaborated or cooperated on academic programmes to begin to agree to a joint programme in Women's Studies.

Programme Governance and Structure

The MA in Women's Studies takes advantage of the resources and expertise which in combination Mount Saint Vincent University, Dalhousie University, and Saint Mary's University are able to provide. A student will apply to one of the three universities and be accepted on the recommendation of a joint body called the Graduate Admissions and Program Committee (GAPC). The student will formally be registered at one university, but will be able to take courses offered at any of the three universities.

Enrolments will be small, with a maximum of nine new full-time and nine new part-time students each year across the three universities. In Nova Scotia, part-time students are assumed to take three years for a one year programme, so at full capacity we might expect to have 27 students at various stages of thesis and course work.

Faculty from all three universities will be able to participate in the programme as supervisors, committee members, or course instructors. Faculty will be invited to apply from the three universities for cross-appointment to the MA graduate programme. Essentially these will be faculty who have regular appointments teaching in Women's Studies, faculty who currently teach in the undergraduate programmes in Women's Studies, and faculty from other units of each university who either teach or do research in areas that draw on feminist expertise. At latest count, there were more than 50 faculty members from the three campuses, most with PhDs, teaching and or doing research in areas pertinent to the MA in Women's Studies. In the hope that all local and regional resources would be available to the students, faculty from other universities in the region will be eligible to be appointed as Adjunct Professors to the programme, and a representative from this group will serve on GAPC.

Teaching and student co-ordination and supervision will be borne equally by the three universities. GAPC will oversee all aspects of the programme: selecting students, making scholarship recommendations, approving supervisors and thesis topics, appointing members of the Women's Studies programme faculty, and so forth. The membership of GAPC will consist of two faculty members each from Mount Saint Vincent, Dalhousie and Saint Mary's, and one Adjunct Professor. The position of Chair of GAPC will rotate annually among the three universities.

The cost of the programme will be shared equally among the three universities. These costs include staff costs, operating expenses, and some resources associated with secretarial services, as well as release time for faculty who will be teaching graduate courses, and for the administrators and Chair of GAPC.

Feminist Spaces in Programme Content

The joint MA is a five credit programme. The compulsory core includes a half class in feminist theory, a half class in feminist methodology, and a graduate seminar. The electives will be courses appropriate to Women's Studies and feminist analysis that students may take from other departments, including additional courses in theory or methods, or directed study courses.

We are striving to create a different space in the academy for different kinds of academic work. In that regard, we believe that it is important to offer some stand-alone Women's Studies classes, classes that are not simply crosslisted from offerings in other departments. In this way, we want to create, at least in part of our programme, the possibility of academic work that does not simply replicate the traditions of the academy, but forges something new and richer.

The Graduate Seminar is key to creating feminist spaces, and is a compulsory part of the joint MA programme. This seminar is rooted in Women's Studies' historical connections to the feminist community in Halifax and in Nova Scotia and reflects our determination to keep Women's Studies in the academy grounded in its original impetus, the women's movement. It will be a space for students to discuss research proposals as well as to integrate material that they encounter in their other courses. But more unusual, and most important for the creation of feminist space, is that this seminar will require each student to participate in field-based learning, and hence to have experience with the women's movement and community-based activity.

This community-based activity is not meant as either a practicum or a research project. The intent is to build on what we typically know about graduate students doing feminist work; they often are involved as volunteers in crisis centres, transition houses, Planned Parenthood, abortion clinics, organizing feminist film festivals, social action groups, working in feminist bookstores, and so on. The seminar would support students in these sorts of community-based activities if such activities are already in place, and would help connect students with community women's movement activities if they have come from other parts of the province or country. The Graduate Seminar would thus provide a forum for students to connect with women's real experiences and issues, to discover what information and knowledge is needed for social change, and to reflect on the relation between the women's movement and the academy and between theory and practice, on issues of power and privilege associated with education, and on the ways feminist theories make sense in light of the realities students will experience in their community involvement.

Currently, there are ongoing projects in the Nova Scotia region where models for this sort of work are developing. One example is Women's FishNet. Three Nova Scotian CRIAW members, including one academic, formed a larger committee to organize Nova Scotia Women's FishNet after they returned from the 1993 CRIAW conference in Newfoundland and the ad hoc Atlantic Caucus, from which Atlantic Women's FishNet emerged. Since then, Nova Scotia Women's FishNet has begun to work with women in fishing communities to identify a number of the problems with current and planned government policies that have ignored women and will destroy the fabric of their local fishing communities. This project is a continuation of the action research in which a number of us have been engaged over the years in Nova Scotia.

The question of how to create an institutional space and an academic course that can actually carry out these goals is a real challenge. How do we develop our capacity to engage with the community in a way that does not exploit, appropriate, or misuse community members and resources? How do we find a way to actually teach this to students on a short-term basis? How, in a Women's Studies Masters programme, do we develop projects that involve students in the community, on the community's terms, when the students are in the programme for perhaps only a few years? Many community needs require a depth of analysis and ongoing commitment. The Graduate Seminar's challenge is to make strong links with the community, and create a space where activists and academics can work productively together.

Creating Feminist Spaces Among Ourselves: Writing the Proposal

Despite the 1970s and 1980s legacy of mistrust and turf protection among us resulting from our competing institutional university affiliations, the shared history (described above) of community involvement outside the universities forged links among us. These links served as a foundation upon which we began to construct collaborative spaces for Women's Studies.

The evolution of an informal committee in the mid-1980s to work through the establishment of a Women's Studies programme at Dalhousie helped build inter-university connections. Several representatives from Mount Saint Vincent and Dalhousie, with one observer from Saint Mary's, began to meet on a regular basis to talk about ways of cooperating, agreeing, initially, that all three universities warranted Women's Studies undergraduate programmes. Dalhousie received approval to offer a Women's Studies undergraduate major in 1987 and Saint Mary's was granted approval in 1991.[3] In 1989, the informal committee was restructured to include two members each from Dalhousie, Mount Saint Vincent, and Saint Mary's as well as one member from the Nova Scotia College of Art and Design. A feminist at the Atlantic School of Theology also became part of the committee.[4] The committee was subsequently formalized as the Inter-University Women's Studies Committee (IUWSC) with the mandate of reporting at least annually to the metro Halifax Academic Vice Presidents.

Through the IUWSC we began to construct more formal cooperative ventures. We started to coordinate inter-university events such as departmental seminars, and began to produce a collective flyer advertising the "Metro Area" Women's Studies Summer School classes. As we began to negotiate what the MA programme would look like, we had to learn to work through our differences and not dissolve back into our respective institutional "turfs." One of the ways we did this in the proposal-writing stage was to move to a different turf altogether, thereby avoiding the symbolic statement made by doing the proposal development on any one of our campus settings.

The existence of our three universities in the same city, all of which had undergraduate Women's Studies programmes, but none of which had sufficient resources for graduate work, made it both possible and necessary to consider establishing a Masters in Women's Studies in a joint and cooperative way. Institutional affiliations were dissolved in order to establish one programme, with one governing structure, and a degree that will have all three university names on it.

Creating Feminist Spaces in Inter-University Procedures: Getting the Proposal Approved

Early on in the process of constructing the joint MA, if anyone on the IUWSC went to a member of our own senior administration to discuss the MA, our talk tended to focus on individual university interests. This drew us away from our own commitment to work collectively as Women's Studies faculty members. We thus settled on a strategy: whenever a meeting had to be held with members of our university administrations (e.g., the graduate Deans, Academic Vice Presidents, librarians, finance officers, public relations staff), we always met with them as a group. In some respects this strategy served an educative purpose: we wanted them to learn that they actually could be in the same room together and discuss joint inter-university governance, joint admissions, and joint scholarships.

An early meeting with Academic Vice Presidents proved very helpful in obtaining the cooperation of lower levels of bureaucracy. We presented the Academic Vice Presidents with our preliminary proposal for a joint programme but with separate degrees. We had worked out an elaborate structure to determine which university was going to grant the degree because we thought having a joint degree would be a problem for the three universities. The three Vice Presidents looked at this structure and said, "This is too complicated. Why not just make it a joint degree?" We have used this example many, many times subsequently to illustrate how easy it was to begin our collaboration. However, had we not spent months working out the structure, cumbersome though it might have been, we suspect the Academic Vice Presidents would never have come up with a collaborative solution.

It was important that we continued to work in this absolutely collaborative way. An example was the review of library resources at the three institutions. Instead of each university doing a separate review, the IUWSC met the librarians collectively and asked them to jointly review the three libraries' collections. We also managed to persuade the graduate studies administrators at each university to conduct the required proposal review, not separately through each university's procedures, but rather through a joint review process, with a committee comprised of two members from each institution. Such shifts to joint action took considerable negotiation.

One area of real difficulty has been the issue of raising money for scholarships. Individual universities have their own particular constituencies, their own sources of funding. To encourage them to think about how to cooperate and develop not only new sources of funding but a new location for that money when it arrives has been a real challenge. For example, how do we establish a body, agency, or mechanism through which scholarships can be administered? If we had a funding drive under way and people were willing to give donations to the joint MA programme, how should we issue income tax receipts? Who would write up the receipts? If a person gave $300, would she receive a receipt for $100 from each of the three universities? This is an ongoing problem which has yet to be solved.

Reactions from our Patriarchal Institutions

The development of our joint MA, and the collaborative processes it entailed, did not occur in a vacuum. External political and organizational factors set in motion in recent years have had, and will continue to have, an impact on our success in developing the programme and how our programme will be received. The attempt to rationalize and restructure the university system in Nova Scotia has had a particular momentum over the last three and a half to four years, as the government has taken a much more active role in trying to determine whether universities in Nova Scotia should restructure, and what university restructuring will look like. Consequently, some dramatic changes have taken place in our university system.

One form of rhetoric that has become very popular in this period of university restructuring is the rhetoric of cooperation. In order to survive in the present political environment, universities need to cooperate. Although our universities still compete for scarce resources, the rhetoric of cooperation has, in retrospect, legitimized our Joint Women's Studies Programme.

The emphasis on cooperation evident in our joint MA proposal has come to be seen in a very favourable light. In fact, in certain university contexts, our proposal (which predated the province-wide cooperation rhetoric) has been used by our administrators as a model of cooperation. Moreover, our particular programme has been seen as the wave of the future. Certainly, that attitude and approach have been important politically in enabling our proposal to be easily approved by Senates at the different universities. It may have prevented the sort of patriarchally based criticisms that have been raised on some university campuses when new Women's Studies programmes are proposed.

However, as our educational system in Nova Scotia is changing rapidly, that rhetoric may promote pragmatism ahead of programme quality. Under those circumstances, the joint Masters' cooperative emphasis can be used to encourage the development of other cooperative programmes, whether or not there are actually grassroots initiatives to develop those programmes. We have always maintained the position, based on our experience, that cooperation and collaboration only effectively work from the ground up among people who truly want to cooperate and work together. Recently, however, we have been seeing in Nova Scotia a form of cooperation enforced by government and university administrations, that is, a "top down" approach.

When we first started to work on the MA, none of our administrators knew we were doing it and they could not have cared less about the plans of women on campus. However, now that there is enforced cooperation amongst programmes throughout our universities, university administrators seem to have forgotten that we have had five years' experience working this out.

Our new invisibility became evident at a recent workshop put together for department chairs from several Halifax universities. Representatives from five American colleges—Amherst, Mount Holyoke, Smith, University of Massachusetts, and Hampshire were invited to this workshop to show universities in Nova Scotia how to create more collaborative programmes. The process and model of the joint MA in Women's Studies, an excellent example of women's knowledge, were totally ignored by organizers of this workshop.

This workshop was intended for universities in Halifax which were working on the model of partnership at that time. Consequently, the discussions with the five colleges' representatives involved Mount Saint Vincent University, Saint Mary's University, the Nova Scotia College of Art and Design and the Atlantic School of Theology. Dalhousie University was not included because it was promoting a merger model at that time.[5] Therefore, only two of us, representing departments at our respective universities, were invited to the meeting to "learn" how to develop a cooperative model, something we had already accomplished with our joint MA in Women's Studies!

Conclusion

Creating feminist spaces has come to have multiple meanings for us. It means working across institutional barriers and historical divisions. It means working on new processes within our institutions so that joint ventures can be undertaken through truly collaborative procedures at all levels. It means creating a graduate programme where students and faculty can engage in doing things differently. It means continuing to understand that the feminist spaces we create in universities are radically indebted to women's community movements, and that we must keep that rootedness at the centre of any ongoing creation of feminist spaces. We have also learned that creating feminist spaces is an ongoing activity, both to maintain spaces already developed, and to open new ones. This is difficult as times get tougher.

In the implementation of our joint MA, we are ready to begin to move beyond the governance matters and start to pay attention to creating feminist spaces for our students through the kind of programme we create. This phase may be the most exciting and will undoubtedly present its own set of challenges.

Footnotes

[1]In developing this proposal and this paper, we have consistently used this order—i.e., the chronological order in which the universities obtained undergraduate programmes in Women's Studies. When we use the word "we" sometimes it is a "we" of the three authors, and sometimes it is a "we" of the programme developers: from Mount Saint Vincent are Pat Baker, Sheva Medjuck, Frances Early, Jane Gordon, and Rhoda Zuk; from Dalhousie: Ann Manicom, Marjorie Stone, and Jane Parpart; and from Saint Mary's: Linda Christiansen-Ruffman, Martha MacDonald, and Gillian Thomas. Shelly Finson, from the Atlantic School of Theology, was also a member of the IUWSC while the programme was being developed.

[2]In 1991-92 we formally agreed to proceed with proposal development and wrote the proposal. The next year, 1992-93, the proposal was discussed, revised, and finally approved at the department level at each of the three universities. In 1993-94, the proposal was reviewed by a graduate level joint review committee and approved at the graduate programme level. The proposal then went through the Senates of each of the Universities between winter 1994 and winter 1995. Finally, it was approved by the Maritime Provinces Higher Education Commission in 1995-96.

[3]Women's Studies teaching, of course, began much earlier and in 1983 there was discussion and even a written draft for an Atlantic Canadian graduate programme in Women's Studies.

[4]The Nova Scotia College of Art and Design and the Atlantic School of Theology both offered feminist courses, although they had no intention of establishing BAs in Women's Studies.

[5]Universities in Nova Scotia have been struggling to respond to the government imperative of rationalization without having the government impose an undesirable model on them. The six post-secondary institutions in the Halifax area proposed different models. Some subscribed to a model of cooperation among autonomous institutions, and others subscribed to a merger model that would have led to fewer institutions altogether. Subsequently all universities have presented what they call a Consortium Model to the government. It is not yet clear how this will change the structure of post-secondary institutions in the Halifax area.

*Ann Manicom has since been relocated to Mount Saint Vincent University.

Graduate Women's Studies in the Heartland

Breaking Ground for a PhD Programme in Women's Studies at the University of Iowa

Florence E. Babb
Women's Studies Programme and Department of Anthropology,
University of Iowa

I currently chair the Women's Studies Programme at the University of Iowa and have a joint appointment in the Anthropology Department. I will describe our Women's Studies Programme and our recent efforts to design a PhD, as well as reflect on my involvement in building a Feminist Anthropology PhD specialization in my other department. I want to describe both areas of my involvement at the university as a way of exploring questions that may be common to many of us who are concerned with graduate feminist education.

Iowa's Women's Studies Programme began in 1973 with a single office and a single half-time faculty appointment. Graduate students played a key role in the early years in teaching such core courses as Introduction to Women's Studies and Feminist Theory. When I was hired in 1982, there was still only one joint appointment in the programme, but a much wider number of faculty were teaching cross-listed courses and several served on the governing board. As a junior faculty member, I was recruited to serve as chair after just one year at Iowa, and I was greatly relieved when we hired Margery Wolf as our second appointment two years later. Margery remains the senior faculty member in the Women's Studies Programme and has also played an instrumental role in getting the Feminist Anthropology Programme off the ground. From Margery's arrival in 1985 through the present, we have added four more joint appointed faculty (all but one through searches that originated in Women's Studies).

Once we began to reach a reasonable size, we began talking about whether to propose a degree programme. We teach a large number of students, but at present offer only a minor at the undergraduate level. We have been reluctant to plan an undergraduate major because of our concern that we might not be able to advise adequately the many students who might approach us. We are already stretched very thin in our joint appointments. It might seem improbable that we would decide to go directly for a PhD programme, but our reasoning was that we now have the critical number of faculty to work with a small number of students at the graduate level. In part, we were motivated by the other two regents institutions in the state of Iowa: Iowa State had recently approved a BA in Women's Studies and the University of Northern Iowa had just proposed and put in place an MA in Women's Studies. Not to be left behind, the University of Iowa sought to take its place in the forefront as the centre for graduate liberal arts education in the state.

After some deliberation, a committee drew up a proposal which we submitted to our graduate college in the fall of 1994. In our proposal, we laid out some newly designed core courses that we would require of our students. They include a first-year seminar to acquaint students with faculty and research in our Women's Studies Programme, two foundation courses offering theory, research, and analysis (one taught by a faculty member in the humanities and the other from the social sciences), a course in the histories of feminisms, a feminist pedagogy course, a practicum, and a seminar for students writing dissertations. In addition, we require three courses in what we call a "diversity" component, and six courses in a single discipline, for methodological strength.

As proposed, this PhD programme would have been the first in the United States in "Feminist Studies." I recall the discussions we had over naming the new doctoral programme. Would it be a PhD in Women's Studies, in line with the name of our programme? Would it be Gender Studies to signal that we want to understand gender as a relationship and socially constructed, or Feminist Theory to attract the "serious" students? We settled on Feminist Studies because it suggests our interest in taking a feminist perspective in any number of directions, not simply looking at women or gender, but in examining aspects of daily life, world politics, cultural theory, and so on. Moreover, we felt it signaled our political commitment to feminism as a movement as well as a scholarly philosophy. Although we expected that naming the programme "Feminist Studies" might raise eyebrows in committees that were required to approve our proposal, we believed this focus would further distinguish our programme as well as reflect the future of gender studies.

In this regard, it is notable that the University of Iowa currently offers a PhD specialization in Feminist Anthropology. Housed entirely within the

Anthropology Department, it is the only such specialized degree in the country. Several faculty in the department, including Margery Wolf and myself (both joint appointments with Women's Studies), began talking about developing a specialization in 1987, and by 1989 we accepted a few students in the programme. The process of offering this specialized curriculum meant only persuading our colleagues in the department, not a complex administrative apparatus. Even so, it took some doing in a department of "independent" thinkers, some of whom were already nervous about the students that we were attracting. Our colleagues grudgingly agreed to announce the specialization at the same time that the more easily acceptable specialization in economic anthropology was being announced (that programme has since been phased out). When it came to naming the programme, our colleagues were more comfortable with "The Anthropology of Gender," but again reluctantly agreed to our argument that "Feminist Anthropology" was more inclusive of what we would set out to do. Students in this programme take core courses in feminist anthropological theory, feminist perspectives on biology and culture, language and gender, and then choose from such electives as feminist ethnography, anthropologies and sexualities, and gender and development studies.

Now that we have had a number of students enter the programme and receive MAs, and a few who are doctoral candidates, it has been interesting to see that some of the strongest graduate students in the Anthropology Department at Iowa—by any measure—are the feminist students. Nevertheless, a few colleagues continue to hold the view that such a specialization is unnecessary when all students eventually specialize anyway ("why a separate programme? it's divisive"). This may well be a reaction to the discomfort they feel with so many self-assured women attracted to the programme—a number of them open lesbians. Despite the doubts occasionally raised by our less adventurous colleagues, however, I would say that the department remains a congenial one for both feminist faculty and students.

At a time when the field of anthropology has been undergoing some significant upheaval, and our own department has wrestled with the question of whether to maintain traditional requirements for graduate students, we argued successfully for allowing our feminist anthropology students greater flexibility in their programmes. Certain feminist courses are required along with other core courses, but students with adequate preparation may specialize sooner. Basing a feminist programme within a single disciplinary department has certain advantages to offer students, including the structure of an established programme, training in the theory and method of a single field, an emphasis on difference as central to anthropology's mission, and the likely prospect of an academic job after graduation. On the other hand, we must coexist with other colleagues and students who are not always convinced of the validity of the feminist specialization.

That brings us back to our Women's Studies Programme proposal for a doctoral degree, which grows out of the feminist commitment to build truly interdisciplinary programmes that are freed from the conventional limitations set by the disciplines. We have long maintained that we need autonomous programmes to meet the needs of feminist scholars, and that to really see the field of Women's Studies advance, we need the space in which to see our work thrive. When teachers and students have that space, a scholarly community can grow and support women who are coming along. Yet, of course, no programme in the university is truly autonomous and we are always seeking the cooperation of others.

This has been put to the test at the University of Iowa over the last few years. In fall 1995, our administration persuaded the Women's Studies Programme that we should change our proposed degree programme to a PhD in "Women's Studies." We did not take the decision easily, for the reasons given before. We wanted our name to reflect our strong commitment to feminist scholarship and practice. But we understood that even if our Dean and Provost supported a need for "feminist" studies, our state's conservative Board of Regents—which must give final approval to new programmes at state universities—would likely be alarmed by the name. We kept our principles intact in the text of the proposal, but changed the name.

Still, we were taken by surprise when we discovered in spring 1996 that we had faculty colleagues at the university who were set against our instituting a doctoral programme. While their petition to delay the decision was phrased in terms of institutional goals and resources, it became clear in later discussions that many opposed awarding the advanced degree in the field of Women's Studies ("why not men's studies?" one colleague fumed). Nevertheless, after two years successfully moving through committees in the university's Graduate College and Provost's Office, the proposal for a PhD in Women's Studies was to come up for a vote by faculty members on May 1, 1996. Unfortunately, the organized opposition was able to prevent the vote from taking place that day by calling for a quorum. We had been alerted only that morning to the petition that was circulating, yet managed to draw out more faculty to the meeting than ever before. But when the quorum was called by a faculty member (something that had never occurred before), the vote was precluded. Now we anticipate that the quorum rule will be changed and our proposal brought back for a vote in late fall 1996.

While we are chastened by the new realization that after almost a quarter century Women's Studies is still unwelcome to a vocal minority on our campus, we are also confident that our many allies will see that the proposal gets a strong show of support the next time it is brought before the graduate faculty of our institution. Then the proposal must go on to its final review by the Iowa State Board of Regents.

Some further questions that we still need to consider seriously in a new PhD programme are: what admissions policy will encourage a diverse pool of applications for a very small number of openings? How can our faculty avoid burn-out when we have promised new core graduate courses, close advising of doctoral students, etc., and we are already exhausted before we begin? Can we maintain a commitment to both theory and practice, interdisciplinary scholarship and disciplinary strength? Will we have the resources to give students advanced training in feminist scholarship that is attentive to race, class, sexual orientation, nationality, and so on? Can we provide graduate students with a "safe space" in which to prepare for academic and other employment, or will they be called upon to defend the terrain of feminist studies on our campus and beyond in the years ahead?

Are we "breaking new ground" with this doctoral programme in Women's Studies? As feminists, we have long recognized a need for a place of our own, where we can take some risks and gain some ground. The heartland of America (as it is so fondly called) may seem an unlikely place in which to find graduate Women's Studies growing stronger. But we are hopeful that students with interests as diverse as postcolonial studies, feminist cultural studies, feminist ethnography, and racial and sexual identity, will come to Iowa and help us create a space where feminist scholarship can flourish.

Struggling with Questions

The Crisis
in Legitimacy

Thelma McCormack
Institute for Social Research, York University

 he tension between visions and realities, between a future goal and the constraints of the present, between the perfect world we imagine and the daily turmoil of "becoming" is part of the human condition, but it is more easily understood at the individual or organizational level than at the abstract, academic level of creating knowledge. We have theory and metatheory, modernism and postmodernism, "culture wars" and "science wars" but at some more grounded level there is uncertainty. How do we know we have set the right agenda? How can we be sure we have found the appropriate discourse? How can we make certain that we have not limited ourselves by rules of logic and methodology in ways that neither deepen our knowledge nor empower us?

These and similar questions hover over us in these early years as we slowly develop a body of knowledge, and the language and strategies for transmitting it. We are uniquely fortunate at York University in having a critical mass of advanced students and faculty with whom we can work collectively or apart to clarify our thinking in classrooms and seminars. For even in the most authoritarian and hierarchical context, teaching is interactional, a form of communication with others that is modifying, if not self-correcting, and at times punishing. Nevertheless, it is out of this communicative give-and-take, that we arrive at a shared understanding, a constructed reality through a process which sociologists call "consensual validation."

But the world of courses, classes, and seminars which brought us together has also divided us. Women scholars who share the same vision, may not share the same reality, while others emphasize the means and the liberatory possibilities of the moment. Oppression, they say, is embedded in the daily routines and bureaucratic structures of our educational processes; if they are contested when they are first encountered, the end will take care of itself. Most feminist scholars fall somewhere between these polarities, but no matter where we stand and what our politics are, we are drawn simultaneously or sequentially in both directions, practical realities and utopian visions.

For our purposes the issue is Women's Studies as an academic programme based in a university, using its resources, subject to its degree-granting regulations, accountable to our peers, and ultimately to the community. Within these parameters we have various degrees of freedom, and limited funding, and can do what universities do best: conduct research, teach ourselves and others, and publish or otherwise communicate our findings and ideas.

In a very short time Women's Studies as a programme and as a discipline has attracted a group of well-educated gifted scholars who are deeply committed to understanding gendered institutions and gendered relationships. If this diverse group of scholars shares a political belief, it is that a durable lasting equality can only be achieved through a redistribution of the world's resources. Thanks in large part to governments and the women's movement, gender equality has become a measure of human rights; gender inequality is no longer recognized as an imperative of social organization or of human nature. Tolerated, as it sometimes is, it nevertheless lacks legitimacy.

What is problematic for some people is the legitimacy of a university-based Women's Studies programme. We have no past reputation to fall back on, no long list of precedents or symbols of approval. Can we build a feminist scholarship without a feminist theory of knowledge (Nelson; Anderson)? Is feminist knowledge based on established disciplines, or is it necessarily interdisciplinary? If the former, which disciplines? What is the relationship between feminist scholarship and feminist activism, or, more broadly, a theory of social change? Does Women's Studies have legitimacy?

Recently, criticisms have come from insiders and outsiders, friends of Women's Studies and its enemies, scholars in other fields and administrators. Nothing escapes notice. Our courses, research, pedagogy, and our ability and that of our students to meet high levels of excellence have been scrutinized, but few persons have attempted to understand the way our knowledge has developed, and what the deeper philosophical problems are of a fledgling discipline.

Fekete and the Brotherhood

Canadian scholars who at one time complained bitterly about the "chilly climate" for Canadians in our universities and who insisted on correcting this imbalance through affirmative action policies are among those who today have created a "chilly climate" for women and have attempted to discredit women's demands. John Fekete, Professor of Cultural Studies and of English at Trent University has been the most outspoken. In his book *Moral Panic: Biopolitics Rising* he sets the pejorative tone by equating Women's Studies with "biopolitics," a term which has certain resonances with Bosnia and ethnic cleansing. Biopolitics, he writes, is a "new primitivism which promotes self-identification through groups defined by categories of race or sex" (22). Thus women are set up as the narrow parochials without a cosmopolitan world-view, and with little interest in or capacity to generalize, while men are the universalists, heirs to the Enlightenment ,who appeal to reason, claim to meet objective standards, and expect no less of others.

In Fekete's view, the feminist parochials have won. Increasingly, he argues, male professors across Canada have been harassed and victimized by women scholars who take no responsibility for their actions or their reckless charges against their male colleagues, while university administrators who are more concerned with damage control than academic freedom look the other way. Fekete claims that research hastily assembled and based on anecdotal evidence is cited to "prove" the case against these men who are some of the most respected in their fields. Having done nothing that is not part of the civil culture of the campus, some men (all men potentially) have become, he suggests, the victims of feminists who insist erroneously that they, not the men, are the victims. It is an Orwellian lie that has paid off in terms of appointments, promotions, research grants, and other perks. At the very least, it has produced an unhappy campus, an environment of suspicion and silence.

Whatever Fekete's intentions were in *Moral Panic: Biopolitics Rising* he has convinced some that they are under siege. Beyond this, however, is his scenario which confuses sex and gender, the former an ascribed category, a question of chromosomes, the latter as learned behaviour which includes a socially acquired language and set of roles. Further, he fails to grasp the powerful nature of gender asymmetricality. Very few women would deny that their lives are defined by a system of inequality which puts them at a disadvantage. Without ever having heard the term "patriarchy" they can tell countless stories and recall many incidents which demonstrate differential privilege along the gender axis. When these two fallacies are combined—confusing sex and gender, and the inability to recognize the stratification of our society based on gender—Fekete loses credibility with women.

Sommers and the Status Quo

Fekete's tone is deliberately provocative, but not likely to impress the converted. A more disturbing set of critical observations has come from a group of women who have a close knowledge of the literature in Women's Studies and, in some instances, have been affiliated with programmes.

"*Who Stole Feminism?*" Christina Hoff Sommers asks. Sommers, an Associate Professor of Philosophy at Clark University, shares many of Fekete's criticisms although not his biological reductionism. Instead, she distinguishes between *equity* feminism and *gender* feminism. Equity feminists, she says, "believe that American women have made great progress and that our system of government allows them to expect more. They do not," she says, "believe that women are 'socially subordinate.' By contrast, gender feminists believe that modern women are still in thrall to patriarchy.... When equity feminists point to the gains made by women in recent decades, gender feminists consider them naive" (250).

The distinction between equity feminism and gender feminism is less about various versions of feminist thinking than it is about social change. Equity feminism, as she explains it, is based on a consensus model of the state, and on a gradualist, incremental process of social change. Gender feminism, on the other hand, is based on a conflict theory of the state, and a political struggle to achieve limited gains. Of course, both kinds of feminism can co-exist within a university, and do, but the difference between them frames research and practice, and is particularly relevant for social policy. To put that in the context of "visions and reality," is our vision a slowly eroding patriarchal order through an electoral and judicial system? Is it a peaceful withering away of a system with deeply entrenched interests in maintaining itself? Or is it a more radical transformation of all social relationships—education, work, family, the state?

Raising Standards by Defusing Politics

The question about the process of social change as gradualism or radical transformation is, in part, answered by how we design curricula, whether we emphasize a discipline-based knowledge—Women and Literature in the English Department—or an interdisciplinary model of knowledge which crosses the discipline lines. In *Professing Feminism*, Daphne Patai, Professor of Women's Studies and of Brazilian Literature at the University of Massachusetts, and Noretta Koertge, Professor of History and Philosophy of Science at the University of Indiana, raise this same question among others. Patai and Koertge consider "identity politics" the crux of the problem: "The logical result of extreme identity-based politics is tribalism or balkanization, the partitioning of a complex system into small ethnically and culturally distinct units of homogeneous identity, none of which seeks coalition with any other unit…" (72).

They have in mind the fragmentation of feminist programmes and organizations, particularly around issues of sexual orientation and colour. In fact, mainstream feminism has been challenged by the need for greater diversity and inclusivity in course content as well as student body and teaching faculty.

However, the politics of diversity and inclusivity is one thing; the scholarship, another, for we have learned the hard way about our own limitations. Patai seems to be less aware of our self-imposed and culture-bound restrictions. She thinks it is only a matter of ideology. But if we look back at the last few years, at the exploration of sexuality and the critique of biomedical models of normal and deviant sexuality, we can see the truly major changes in our assumptions about human nature. At present only the surface has been touched, but the theories and hypotheses will keep us engaged for another century, while the demonstrations, lobbying, and court cases have picked up momentum. Still, not all women enrolled in our courses are interested in same-sex relations, or regard this as a priority or the cutting edge of contemporary scholarship. On the contrary, they are uncomfortable with it and what they sense as a coercive environment unsympathetic to their "straight" values.

The in-your-face style of inclusivity politics has been divisive and left a trail of bitter feelings in the movement as well as academe. Any illusions about solidarity were shaken. Patai and Koertge use this divisiveness as a springboard for their most serious charge: that the new feminist scholarship is intended not to teach, not to make women more critical of stereotypes and received wisdom, not to educate them to compare hypotheses or interpretations, but to mobilize them, to recruit them for a new ideology. Women's Studies professors, they claim, are deliberately using classrooms as sites for training students to become feminist activists. The rewards go to do-ers not thinkers.

This kind of activity may, they concede, help the movement but it undermines the university as an institution and deeply compromises knowledge. What we must do, they say, is restore the status of value-free knowledge as an end in itself and reposition Women's Studies in traditional disciplines where the norms of professionalism still prevail. We need, furthermore, to go back to a more conventional curriculum and a scholarship removed from ideologies and inflammatory rhetoric that stimulate and sustain praxis.

The pluralistic liberal model, they believe, provides better scholarship, better mentoring, and is a more hospitable environment than the advocacy environment of a separate Women's Studies programme. "It is high time progressive women and men stopped waxing sentimental about both the plight and the latent virtues of the oppressed and started exercising a little tough-minded common sense in proposing realistic workable reforms" (Patai and Koertge 81).

If we were to follow their reasoning and advice, Women's Studies would be less visible in the university and safely marginalized within traditional disciplines where it would be held accountable by departments—English, History, Anthropology, Psychology, Language Studies—and judged by their norms. An interdisciplinary programme would become a minor exception, a token gesture to look "politically correct" and defuse any militant protest. Meanwhile, the fate of Women's Studies would be tied to the fate of the older disciplines.

Interdisciplinary studies has a different intellectual rationale. Patai and Koertge are not interested in pursuing this, and the truth is, that many of us who are committed to interdisciplinary models have not made a strong case. The best of our feminist journals provide a mix of articles in the social sciences, humanities, and science, but authors almost never cross disciplines and very seldom do two persons of different disciplines work together. The promise of greater reciprocity remains only a promise, and on a practical level we provide no rationale to our universities for creating a special unit, for giving us our own domain.

The trade-off is standards, for if we have made little progress toward a new, genuinely interdisciplinary knowledge, it cannot be said that our standards have been lowered to satisfy marginal students, or to build up the self-esteem of women who have experienced the discrimination of the system. Excellence indeed has been the norm. Where women attempt to build an interdisciplinary analysis, the standards are intuitive, and unspecified, and many have felt the need to develop a different kind of standard. Meanwhile, there is abundant evidence in our libraries and bookstores, in science labs and in art galleries to feel confident that the most rigorous standards are being maintained.

Indeed, contrary to the fears of Patai and Koertge and others, the risk is not a decline in standards but feminist elitism. Few of us can resist the pleasures of being invited to give keynote addresses to our professional organizations, the validation one feels from seeing a publication in a strictly refereed journal, the euphoria of seeing yourself cited by your colleagues. These are seductive and must be weighed against the demeaning slurs—"Is this really a course?" "All attitude!" "Therapeutic knowledge for the walking wounded"—that we often confront in courses that are interdisciplinary. In short, the mission to develop interdisciplinary studies can fail for two reasons: the standards are not sufficiently high, and the standards are too high. Critics, among them Patai and Koertge understand the first; many of us understand the second.

Rescuing Women's Studies from Postmodernism and Sameness

Interdisciplinary studies owes much to postmodernism's dissatisfaction with a canon that restricted how far we could stray from the prescribed problems and their formats. Postmodernism opened the door to new feminist interpretations of old texts. To some, this looked like anarchy. In *Feminism Without Illusions*, Elizabeth Fox-Genovese, Professor of Humanities and of History at Emory , formerly Director of Women's Studies, focuses on the negative impact of postmodernism on Women's Studies. In *Feminism Without Illusions*, she argues that postmodernism is the contemporary, post-liberal version of individualism, and deprives us, she says, of a common culture. In addition, its lack of discrimination undermines rational discourse.

All knowledge, she argues, requires a canon just as all societies require rules. To deny the canon is, she says, to give women no basis for self-discipline, and, moreover, diminishes the enriched experience that reflects a civilization. Yet, she recognizes that to accept the canon is to internalize a whole system of repression which excludes women from achieving greatness, diminishes them as scholars, and, effectively, silences them. Either way, agency eludes them.

Feminist scholars who have deconstructed the canon and exposed its phallocentric biases have not, she says, created an alternate canon. Ironically, as Fox-Genovese explains, the "new" canon is a mirror image of the old where women are seen as different, as more nurturing, more concerned with others. "Most feminist scholars," she says, "in their determination to expose the canon's and our culture's androcentrism, have protested the ways in which they have denied women's political and cultural authority but have then turned around and constructed a feminist theory that disconcertingly represents women in the same terms that the canon represented them" (1991, 181).

Postmodernism reinvents the *tabula rasa*, a space, a salon where everyone's story, male or female, present or past, western or non-western, can claim validation. As a result of this extreme individualism there is no basis for a common women's culture that could support a collective identity. Thus, she concludes, we cannot abandon the canon or its history; we can only reform and modify it.

The reform or modification that Fox-Genovese envisages idealizes the two-parent nuclear family, and questions the secularization of social life that separates sex and morality. She maintains that by disaggregating any kind of social unit, individualism leads to a definition of equality as sameness where men and women become interchangeable. According to her argument, equality means that there is no basis for discrimination, no basis for a gendered division of labour, no basis for exclusion or segregation.

Feminists who have advocated equality, Fox-Genovese says, run counter to women's special biological constitution, their function in reproduction, and tie to the family. "[For] individualism has proved incapable of coming to terms with the most fundamental aspect of our humanity—the sexual difference that permits us to reproduce ourselves as a species" (1991, 160).

Contemporary feminist theory has reached an impasse between equality as sameness and the recognition and valorization of difference. Postmodernism, she suggests, negates both. "Thus feminism, which began with the attempt to claim for women the rights that men were proclaiming for themselves, is moving irrationally and at high political risk toward the repudiation of any notion of right beyond that of personal experience" (1991, 153).

Most feminists would agree with her criticism of individualism, or, at least, of classical liberal individualism. She is also correct in thinking that without a shared culture and a common historical memory we are unable to develop a collective consciousness and become a social movement. Furthermore, she has picked up on the anti-natalism that runs through much of Anglo-American feminist thinking on reproductive policies. That having been said, very few feminists would agree with her assertions that equality is equivalent to sameness, and, that difference is defined by reproductive functions.

Biology does make women different from men, though not as different as dimorphic models of sexuality have led us to believe. But it is the meaning we attach to this difference and its relevance for participation in public life that are the issues that have framed feminist theory and informed Women's Studies. The phrase women marched to, "biology is not destiny," was more than political rhetoric. It was a reminder of past history when sexual intercourse was a form of conjugal duty, and too many pregnancies left women so exhausted in body and mind that they were barely able to realize their potential privately or publicly.

In *Feminism is Not the Story of My Life* Fox-Genovese returns to the difference theme and goes further, also deploring not only the ideal of individualism, but the ethos of secularization that separates morality from human sexuality. In particular, she is critical of our thinking about abortion, and makes the extraordinary statement that feminists have not been as eager to free themselves from men as from babies. "The official feminist position," she writes, "continues to be primarily driven by two convictions: first, that women should not be forced to marry in order to have children, and, second, that children do not need relations with parents of both sexes" (1996, 235). This is the language of "family values" politics, of Newt Gingrich, and the voice of anti-secularists who believe that all complicated social problems can be resolved by reference to a simple morality.

Fox-Genovese is so disturbed about the "welfare" family headed up by a single woman, that she regards the idea of orphanages as less undesirable. By idealizing the two-parent nuclear family as the norm and pathologizing the single-parent family she undoes all the work feminists have accomplished in recognizing the diversity of family structures in our communities, including same-sex families. But it is strange for a social historian to be making these statements, for she must recognize that the nuclear family is an historical phenomenon, a way of organizing an individualistic, competitive economy. She thus joins the ranks of conservative thinkers, not just about the family as a single microsystem, but also about the relationship of morality to social policy. Perhaps this is why the title of her recent book is *Feminism is Not the Story of My Life*.

Two Versions of Legitimacy

Let me conclude with the question I raised at the start. Does our enterprise have legitimacy? If it does not enjoy an everyday common sense legitimacy, can we make truth claims for it? When educated people say, "according to psychologists," or "according to economists," or "according to biologists," can we say, "according to feminists" and have it mean something? Can we claim resources for it if we are constantly being discredited by our colleagues whose model of a discipline is based on conventional scholarship?

Feminist studies is new and dissident, and like other unfamiliar disciplines it is vulnerable. Left and right, feminists and anti-feminists, educational radicals and educational conservatives have assumed adversarial positions. Thus, the question of legitimacy assumes a larger place than if women scholars and Women's Studies had more time and a more leisurely development. Difficult issues that remain on the table include whether we have a theory of knowledge, what we mean by social change, whether our work is necessarily interdisciplinary, and how far we can or should accommodate students who feel they are being pushed too far too fast, or those who feel we are not radical enough.

The critics discussed here make legitimacy depend on a conservative vision, academic business-as-usual. If our vision is bolder, we may have to settle for two versions of legitimacy, a hard one acquired through rigorous quantitative and qualitative methods, and based on a canon, and another "softer" one based on what Robert Bellah calls "habits of the heart."

References

Anderson, Elizabeth. "Feminist Epistemology: An Interpretation and a Defense." *Hypatia* 10.3 (Summer 1995): 50-83.

Bellah, Robert N. *Habits of the Heart.* New York: Harper and Row:1985.

Fekete, John. *Moral Panic: Biopolitics Rising.* Montreal: Robert Davies, 1975.

Fox-Genovese, Elizabeth. *Feminism Without Illusions.* Chapel Hill: University of North Carolina, 1991.

Fox-Genovese, Elizabeth. *Feminism is Not the Story of My Life.* New York: Doubleday, 1996.

Nelson, Lynn Hankinson. "The Very Idea of Feminist Epistemology." *Hypatia* 10.3 (Summer 1995): 31-49.

Patai, Daphne, and Noretta Koertge. *Professing Feminism: Cautionary Tales from the Strange World of Women's Studies.* New York: Basic, 1994.

Sommers, Christina Hoff. *Who Stole Feminism?: How Women Have Betrayed Women.* New York: Touchstone, 1995.

In Defense of Discipline-Based Feminist Scholarship

Deborah Gorham
Pauline Jewett Institute of Women's Studies, Carleton University

After nearly three decades of institution building in Women's Studies at the undergraduate level throughout North America, graduate Women's Studies programmes are rapidly emerging in Canada.[1] I assume that most scholars involved in establishing these programmes see them as a logical extension of activity at the undergraduate level and that most assume, to a greater or lesser degree, that Women's Studies represents a new field of knowledge. In this article I present some criticisms of Women's Studies institutionbuilding and raise some questions about the wisdom of encouraging a proliferation of new programmes at the graduate level at Canadian universities.

The origins of the Women's Studies programmes that exist today are to be found in the work of feminist scholars of the late 1960s and early 1970s, many of whom, inspired by their own activist commitment to feminism, began to give courses and to pursue research on women. These scholars had all been trained in particular branches of knowledge—in academic "disciplines"—and many of the courses they first introduced were discipline-based. But soon, courses in Women's Studies, usually defining themselves as interdisciplinary, were established. By the mid-1970s, courses, both discipline-based and interdisciplinary, had proliferated and discussions about the nature and the direction of feminist scholarship were well underway. In the United States, the question of whether or not Women's Studies should be regarded as a new field of knowledge was being hotly debated by the late 1970s. The volume *Theories of Women's Studies*, a collection of essays selected from papers presented at the first National Women's Studies Association (NWSA) Conference, held in 1979 at Lawrence, Kansas, provides a good reflection of one side of this debate. In their introduction, editors Gloria Bowles and Renate Duelli Klein tell us that at that 1979 NWSA conference many participants were asking "if ... Women's Studies was forming itself as an academic discipline, a study in its own right."[2] The articles in *Theories of Women's Studies* answer this question in the affirmative.

One of the strongest pieces in the Bowles and Klein collection is Sandra Coyner's "Women's Studies as an Academic Discipline: Why and How To Do It." Coyner offers an excellent analysis of the origins and significance of the academic disciplines, and presents a cogent case for regarding Women's Studies as a separate academic discipline.

The origins of "the disciplines" are to be found in the development of the modern university in the nineteenth century, which led to the professionalization of scholarship, and the organization of restrictive standards for entry into the scholarly community. As Coyner points out, in the late twentieth-century context "disciplines" are more than simply branches of knowledge; they claim to be distinct "systems of thought including concepts, theories, methods ..." (48).

Coyner quite rightly challenges claims of the traditional disciplines to timeless coherence or to "objectivity," claims that have been used to criticize feminist and other scholars who challenge the scholarly establishment from the margins. She follows up her analysis of the disciplines with a critique of the model of interdisciplinarity as an organizing principle for feminist scholarship. She rejects this model as well, asserting that "our central goal should be to build our own new knowledge" (56). Finally, drawing on Thomas Kuhn's *The Structure of Scientific Revolutions*, Coyner asserts that Women's Studies must begin to think of itself as a discipline and to recognize that it represents "a completely new way of viewing humanity" (54). It represents the formation of a paradigm in the Kuhnian sense.

While I find her arguments impressive, I do not accept all of Coyner's analysis. First, I reject the claim made by Coyner and others that a feminist approach to scholarship *in itself* generates new knowledge or creates new methodologies for research or teaching. Feminism has been a major defining force for most of my adult life. As a set of fundamental beliefs feminism has informed my politics, my personal life and my scholarship. I will not attempt to define feminism here except to say that while I recognize the diversity and complexity of contemporary feminism, I continue to favour the use of the term "feminism" rather than "feminisms" because I believe that there is a core definition to which all feminists can agree. As Rosalind Delmar has put it:

> It is certainly possible to construct a base-line definition of feminism and the feminist which can be shared by feminists and non-feminists. Many would agree that at the very least a feminist is someone who holds that women suffer discrimination because of their sex, that they have specific needs which remain negated and unsatisfied, and that the satisfaction of these needs would require a radical change (some would say a revolution even) in the social, economic and political order. (8)

Because the university remains part of a larger milieu that still resists feminism, being a feminist has made me critical of many of the structures and practices associated with the modern university. Indeed, one of the great achievements of feminists within the academy has been to point out the extent to which modern scholarship has defined itself as an enterprise for and largely about powerful men.

On the other hand, while I define myself as a feminist, I also define myself as a scholar, and for me, feminism is the point of view that informs feminist scholarship. It is not, in and of itself, scholarship. As a feminist scholar I experience an inevitable tension between my identification with the political movement, feminism, and my support as a scholar for the values of scholarship. As scholars on the margins, feminist women do indeed perceive with special clarity the errors, the self-serving qualities, and the prejudices of scholarship, but as a scholar, I am committed to the best of these values which for me as an historian include a commitment to thoroughness, accuracy, and balanced judgment, and an obligation to contextualize. As historian Linda Gordon has said: "It is wrong to conclude, as some have, that because there may be no objective truth possible, there are no objective lies. There may be no objective canons of historiography, but there are degrees of accuracy; there are better and worse pieces of history" (22).

And where are we most likely to maintain that tension, to continually confront, rather than ignore, the challenges of negotiating a path between our feminist convictions and our scholarly work? In most cases, I would suggest, from a position as active but oppositional participants within the "traditional" disciplines. I say this not because I believe that the academic disciplines are carved in stone. As ways of organizing knowledge, academic disciplines are clearly creations of a particular era, and disciplinary divisions are often arbitrary. However, we do need organizing concepts. The academic disciplines of our modern universities offer traditions of knowing and understanding and methodological and theoretical perspectives that have developed over years of debate and discussion. These traditions, flawed though they are, help the feminist scholar to remain grounded in what most scholarship should be about, namely: the reinterpretation and transmission of the knowledge of the past, and the creation of new knowledge.

It is this lack of connection with what I see as the fundamental concerns of scholarship that troubles me about some Women's Studies discourse. For example, in my work for this paper, I read much about the genesis of feminist scholarship and Women's Studies: only rarely in this literature did I encounter an interest in gathering empirical data about our very own history. Canadian sociologist Margrit Eichler has been one of the few people to gather such data, and in a recent piece on the connection between Women's Studies and the women's movement, she notes that while it is "part of our conventional wisdom that Women's Studies have emerged 'out of the women's movement' it seems astonishing that there is, to the best of my knowledge, not a single empirical study that has actually examined (rather than postulated) the relationship between the two" (120).

I am also concerned by what I see as a tendency within Women's Studies itself to diminish the complexity of its own most important issues by resorting to slogans. This is true, for example, of some current discussions within universities of "diversity." One of the most important achievements of late twentieth-century feminism has been the development by working-class women and women of colour of a body of feminist thinking and social practices that sharply question the dominance of white, bourgeois feminist ideology. This thinking is beginning to have powerful effects on feminist research. However, too often, in debates about Women's Studies, in discussions of feminist pedagogy, and in some introductory Women's Studies texts, discourse about race, class, gender, and diversity has become ideological in a formulaic and therefore static way.

For example, that formulaic, predictable response is reflected in the remarks of some of the participants in a 1995 exchange on the Women's Studies Internet List (WMSL) about whether or not Betty Friedan would be an appropriate person to invite as a speaker to university campuses. "I certainly don't believe that she is the best person to invite to speak on the feminist movement," wrote one participant. "I thought we'd moved past middle-class straight, white feminism." Other subscribers, it should be noted, did object to such attacks: "I am sick of hearing about what didn't get said. Visionaries are not necessarily omniscient ... flawless.... If we must judge each moment ... by the harsh and divisive standards of today's multiplicities in feminisms, then we will start over and over.... This time we will have only ourselves to blame."[3] Even the best introductory textbooks in Women's Studies, no less than in other fields, must of necessity resort to the simplification of concepts, but such simplification can encourage thinking of the kind that would simply dismiss Betty Friedan. For example, the recent Canadian feminist reader, *Feminist Issues: Race, Class, and Sexuality*, edited by Nancy Mandell, while admirable in many ways, and certainly sensitive to issues concerning racism, begins with a chapter on "Feminist Theories" which uses what has become the standard but, in my view, simplistic division of feminism into liberal/socialist/radical divisions to which it adds others, including "anti-racist feminism" or "standpoint feminism." Although "critiques" are provided for liberal, socialist, and radical feminism, "standpoint feminism" is presented without such a critique.

In part, this impoverishment is a result of the resurgent backlash against feminism and against what the academic right calls "political correctness," which has polarized debate and, in the United States, especially, caused discourse among feminists and non-feminists to become intensely acrimonious. Partly it is a result of the polarization of debate among feminists themselves.

The acrimony and the weaknesses in the current discourse relating to Women's Studies are reflected in three books about Women's Studies in American universities: *Who Stole Feminism?* by Christina Hoff Sommers; *Professing Feminism*, by Daphne Patai and Noretta Koertge; and *The Feminist Classroom*, by Frances Maher and Mary Tetreault. All were published in 1994, and all have received considerable attention.[4]

Who Stole Feminism?, a tendentious attack on contemporary feminism within and outside the academy, is easy enough to dismiss. Not only is it one-sided and insulting in tone to its opponents, its main point, that academic feminists or "gender feminists" are accomplishing the "feminist colonization of the American academy" is patently false. However, in spite of its offensiveness, I found disturbing grains of truth in what Sommers has to say, for example, about the bureaucratization of feminism and about "feminist pedagogy." These are the themes taken up in *Professing Feminism*, a highly critical assessment of Women's Studies, but a book which should not be confused with *Who Stole Feminism?* Its authors offer some criticisms of "feminist pedagogy" and identity politics to which Women's Studies scholars should be paying attention.

In particular, I think that the authors of *The Feminist Classroom* should have paid attention to criticisms of this kind. *The Feminist Classroom* is a study of the benefits of feminist pedagogy and a celebration of its achievements. I found the book disturbing for several reasons, not least among them the fact that in its discussion of "feminist pedagogy" *The Feminist Classroom* focuses exclusively on issues related to the political significance of interaction in the classroom and with the promotion of race and gender equity. It is not that I find these goals unworthy or unimportant, although I strongly disagree with some of the intentions and methods suggested in this book. I think the authors and their informants are, for example, confused and even disingenuous in their treatment of "authority," an issue to which they devote a chapter. They condemn "traditional" conceptions of academic authority. "Traditionally, professorial authority comes from superior knowledge of the academic discipline; it is lodged in the hierarchical relationship of expert to teacher to student, and enforced institutionally by the power and duty to assign grades" (127) but their method of "positioning students as academic authorities" (130) rests, in my view, on a covert authoritarianism at least as coercive as the "traditional" sort.

But what I find most troubling about *The Feminist Classroom* is that in a book about university teaching, pedagogical issues relating to the teacher's fundamental task of imparting information and fostering clear and complex thinking and writing are virtually excluded. Feminist pedagogy, it seems, is exclusively about feminist politics. *The Feminist Classroom* ignores criticisms like those voiced in *Professing Feminism* concerning both the intellectual content of Women's Studies courses and the negative consequences of some of the techniques of teaching designed to encourage "diversity" and make the classroom a "safe" place for women. Because the authors evade these issues, they avoid the challenge of acknowledging that there may well be a connection between such strategies and the discouraging experiences that many people—myself included—have had with some Women's Studies students in recent years. For example, one Women's Studies student in a history class, who was annoyed with me because I would not say that 9,000,000 women died during the early modern European witch persecutions, flatly rejected my suggestion that she re-read the assigned article, which put the figure at 100,000 or less.[5] She said she saw no reason why she should believe either the scholarly author, or myself, rather than her own sources of information. I know this is only another anecdote, and perhaps this student's unfortunate lack of understanding of the meaning of research had little to do with her status as a Women's Studies student. However, it could be interpreted as a gross misinterpretation of discourse about "positioning students as academic authorities" (130).

In my view, Women's Studies discourse about feminist pedagogy and other matters would benefit from an increased respect for empirical knowledge, which Women's Studies scholars have often viewed with suspicion. In part, this suspicion can be attributed to the fact that many early participants in Women's Studies were part of the 1960s and 1970s critique of the social sciences for what was seen as its positivism, its unexamined attachment to data gathering, objectivity, and categorization. This critique had its value and its importance, but it also has had negative consequences.

Speaking in 1979, Charlotte Bunch, in discussing the limitations of "compensatory" feminist scholarship, pointed out that the "add-women-and-stir-method" was an insufficient agenda for Women's Studies.[6] She made an important point. But now, 17 years later Women's Studies needs once again to acknowledge that empirical research—"adding women"—is essential to the enterprise of feminist scholarship; it takes effort and skill, it is exciting, and it deserves to be treated with respect.

I am not suggesting here a return to unexamined empiricism, nor am I saying that feminist scholarship does not change knowledge, raise questions about methodologies or alter theoretical perspectives. It can and should do all of these. My question is about where best to engage in such scholarship: by asserting a separate place for ourselves? Or by insisting on staying centrally grounded in the existing structures of the university? Clearly, I favour encouraging the latter option as the norm. This is not to say that feminist scholarship does not need institutions of its own, or that we should ignore the importance of interdisciplinarity. I suggest that some development at the graduate level is both beneficial and necessary. The PhD programme at York University seems to me both admirable and important. What worries me is that, unless we think carefully, we will find that all universities in Canada will be forced to establish such programmes, simply because institution building of this kind tends inevitably to reproduce itself.

The question of institution building brings me to my final point, which has more to do with the material circumstances of university life than with the intellectual issues on which I have been focusing. The dangers of the co-optation of feminism have been present since the beginning of the movement for feminist scholarship. The feminist scholars of the early 1970s, for the most part then junior and untenured, were not only challenging the universities, but also needed to be part of the institutions. They needed tenure and then promotion, and their students needed degrees.

In some ways, the establishment of Women's Studies degree programmes has increased the danger of co-optation. While we must indeed struggle to make the voices of feminist scholarship heard in universities, degree programmes may not always be the most effective means to the desired end. The looser, less conventional structures that existed on many campuses before degree programmes were established—Carleton University's Interfaculty Committee on Women's Studies, which was established in 1975 and functioned until it was replaced by the degree programme in 1987 provides a good example— suited feminist scholarship better than the more formal structures that have followed. Degree programmes, in part simply because they create structural obligations to students who enrol in the programme, inevitably enmesh the project of feminist scholarship much more inextricably with the university's bureaucracy than for example would a less formal Centre for Feminist Research. Degree programmes must, for example, mount their "core" courses, even if the teaching resources provided by the university in any given year are simply not sufficient to the task. Too often, the establishment of undergraduate degree programmes has drained energy away from teaching, research, and learning and squandered it in the sisyphian labour of administrating units which are always underfunded and understaffed. It has meant taking energy away from transforming the disciplines and the university as a whole. I fear that a proliferation of freestanding graduate degree programmes in Women's Studies could have the same unfortunate effect.

Footnotes

[1]These include the MA-PhD at York University which admitted its first students in 1992; the new collaborative programme at the University of Toronto; and new MA programmes at Memorial University and the University of Ottawa. As data compiled by the National Women's Studies Association in the U.S. demonstrate, this growth in Canada is part of a continent-wide development; see Humphreys; Kidd and Spencer. Figures cited in both editions about "Women's Studies" graduate programmes should be used with care: the editors tend to conflate Women's Studies with courses on women/ gender in specific disciplines.
[2]The NWSA was founded in San Francisco in 1977. See Boxer, p. 81.
[3]The anti-Friedan participant was Trinity Treat, May 12, 1995. The participant who objected was Miriam Harris, May 12, 1995 (WMSL).
[4]For example they were reviewed together by Carol Sternhell in the December 1994 issue of *The Women's Review of Books*.

[5]The article assigned was William Monter, "Protestant Wives, Catholic Saints, and the Devil's Handmaid: Women in the Age of Reformations," in Renate Bridenthal, Claudia Koonz, and Susan Stuard, (eds.) *Becoming Visible: Women in European History*, (Boston: Houghton Mifflin, 1987).

[6]For Bunch's speech, see Boxer, "For and About Women…" page 90, footnote 81: "The expression 'add-women-and-stir method' was used by Charlotte Bunch in a panel, "Visions and Revisions: Women and the Power to Change" (NWSA Convention, Lawrence, Kansas, June 1979): excerpts were published in *Women's Studies Newsletter* 7(3) (Summer 1979): 20-21."

References

Bowles, Gloria, and Renate Duelli Klein. "Introduction: Theories of Women's Studies and the Autonomy/Integration Debate." *Theories of Women's Studies*. Eds. Gloria Bowles and Renate Duelli Klein. London: Routlege, 1989. First published in 1983.

Boxer, Marilyn J. "For and About Women: The Theory and Practice of Women's Studies in the United States." *Reconstructing the Academy: Women's Education and Women's Studies*. Eds. Elizabeth Minnich, Jean O'Barr, and Rachel Rosenfeld. Chicago: University of Chicago Press, 1988.

Coyner, Sandra. "Women's Studies as an Academic Discipline: Why and How To Do It." *Theories of Women's Studies*. Eds. Gloria Bowles and Renate Duelli Klein. London: Routlege, 1989. First published in 1983.

Delmar, Rosalind. "What is Feminism?" *What is Feminism?: A Re-Examination*. Eds. Juliet Mitchell and Ann Oakley. New York: Pantheon, 1986.

Eichler, Margrit. "Not Always an Easy Alliance: The Relationship Between Women's Studies and the Women's Movement in Canada." *Challenging Times: The Women's Movement in Canada and the United States*. Eds. Constance Backhouse and David H. Flaherty. Montreal and Kingston: McGill-Queen's University Press, 1993.

Gordon, Linda. "What's New in Women's History." *Feminist Studies/Critical Studies*. Ed. Teresa de Lauretis. Bloomington, IN: Indiana University Press, 1986.

Humphreys, Debra. *Guide to Graduate Work in Women's Studies, 1991*. College Park, MD: NWSA, University of Maryland, 1991.

Kidd, Karen, and Adne Spencer, eds. *Guide to Graduate Work in Women's Studies. Second Edition, 1994*. College Park, MD: National Women's Studies Association, University of Maryland, 1994.

Kuhn, Thomas S. *The Structure of Scientific Revolutions*. Second Edition. Chicago: University of Chicago Press, 1970.

Maher, Frances A., and Mary Kay Thompson Tetreault. *The Feminist Classroom: An Inside Look at How Professors and Students are Transforming Higher Education for a Diverse Society*. New York: Basic Books, 1994.

Mandell, Nancy, ed. *Feminist Issues: Race, Class, and Sexuality*. Scarborough: Prentice Hall Canada, 1995.

Patai, Daphne, and Noretta Koertge. *Professing Feminism: Cautionary Tales from the Strange World of Women's Studies*. New York: A New Republic Book, Basic Books, 1994.

Sommers, Christina Hoff. *Who Stole Feminism?: How Women Have Betrayed Women*. New York: Simon and Schuster, 1994.

Sternhell, Carol. "The Proper Study of Womankind." *The Women's Review of Books* 12.3 (1994): 1, 3-4.

Reflections on Crossing Disciplines

Rae Anderson
Department of Social Anthropology, York University

One of the hallmarks of feminist research historically has been its interdisciplinarity. This article reflects upon some of the efforts involved when engaging in such interdisciplinary research.

The term "interdisciplinary" has been used very loosely and broadly, and is at times used interchangeably with other terms such as multi-disciplinary or cross-disciplinary. While there are many who have attempted to define[1] interdisciplinary research, I have found Stember's overview of the terminology very useful.

Stember draws distinctions between *intra-disciplinary* work as research within a particular discipline, and *multi-disciplinary* study which places disciplines side by side, with each discipline providing a different perspective on a particular problem. *Cross-disciplinary* research is represented as an attempt to position the disciplines interrogatively and critically in relation to each other, that is, "viewing one discipline from the perspective of another" (4). According to Stember's typology, *interdisciplinary* research (in its specific sense) involves an integration of several disciplines when they are brought to bear on a particular issue. "Interdisciplinary integration brings interdependent parts of knowledge into harmonious relationship through strategies such as relating part and whole or the particular and the general" (4). *Trans-disciplinary* work involves a fusion or a unity of intellectual frameworks (e.g., critical Marxist approaches) beyond disciplinary perspectives.

All these kinds of interdisciplinarity involve questions about what constitutes a discipline, offer distinctive frames of understanding, and suggest different possibilities for the relationship between disciplines. Interdisciplinarity in all its guises potentially challenges disciplinarity, defined as "an essentialist tendency in the production of academic knowledge that produces a set of theoretical and methodological axioms, and then formalizes them as dogma" (Kavoori 174).

Much of the literature about interdisciplinarity seems to focus on research which involves two or more researchers from more than one discipline working collectively on a problem. Stember, for instance, concentrates particularly upon the group dynamics involved in bringing together interdisciplinary teams in the social sciences.

This article, however, draws upon my experiences as an interdisciplinary, *lone* practitioner, and uses these as a starting point for thinking about the nature of doing interdisciplinary research.

A Testimonial

My Master's thesis in Interdisciplinary Studies examined the relationship between gender and power in masquerade rituals cross-culturally in small-scale societies, through comparative analysis of the ethnographic literature. The research program involved the production of a thesis as well as a series of major installations. I am a visual artist (a mask-maker), and my work encouraged me to re-think how our knowledge is socially constructed, and to consider diverse ways of presenting research.

Feminist scholarship continues to inform much of my research, not only in the sense that my research concentrates upon gender issues, but also because I have embraced the ways of working in feminist theory to examine cultural practices. The spirit of feminist epistemology suggests a broad conception of the construction of knowledge which may include talking, tacit knowledge, and symbolic and aesthetic forms of communication.

My doctoral dissertation in Social Anthropology examined cultural assumptions about the appropriate place for activities of living and working in artists' housing cooperatives—assumptions entrenched in architectural design, urban planning mandates, land use regulations, zoning by-laws, and building codes.

One ongoing theme of this study was to explore the crossing of boundaries, for example, looking across disciplinary boundaries by drawing upon literature from many fields (e.g., Anthropology, Sociology, Environmental Studies,

Psychology, Architecture, Art, Urban Studies, and Women's Studies). There was no attempt to keep the strands of these various concentrations distinct in my writing.

With the doctoral research I brought together my careers as visual artist and as anthropologist, and in the process of writing was very much aware of this "double voiced-ness." The boundaries theme was explored in other ways: through textual study and discourse analysis, spatial analysis, narrative, metaphor, paintings, and photographs. Newspaper articles, architectural drawings, government legislation, minutes of meetings, building code regulations, and funding mandates all provided grist for the analytical mill. The very act of writing up fieldwork can be understood as itself a task analogous to making art. Conscious decisions about what materials to use, what images to concentrate upon, what details to highlight, choice of framing, all have their counterpart in the sculpting of text.[2]

My current research continues around the gendering of urban space and architectural design. The research focuses on housing design issues for homeless women through two case studies of housing for chronically homeless street people in Toronto. As with the doctoral research, this study requires command of numerous fields. Most recently I have had to gain knowledge of the substantial literature on homelessness, and community and mental health literature. The research has been funded under the Strategic Grants Program, Women and Change, of the Social Sciences and Humanities Research Council of Canada. Strategic grants are specifically targeted to encourage *pragmatic, problem-oriented*, and *interdisciplinary* research. That this kind of granting program has been established is an encouraging sign of the recognition of the need for interdisciplinary strategies to address urgent contemporary social issues.

My ongoing interest is in building connections between a number of fields. Anthropology has historically provided a holistic framework for integrating individual agency, institutionalized structures, and environmental constraints. This holistic framework encourages empirical studies, cross-cultural comparison, and a situating of research interests within broader social/cultural contexts. The nature of intra-disciplinary (within discipline) practice in anthropological work is then inherently interdisciplinary. Thus, while I may think of myself as an "interdisciplinarian," I am "disciplined" in the sense of having aligned myself with the discipline of anthropology. I work within that discipline. I am also "undisciplined" in the sense of valuing and looking to other fields and specialties for their insights. I work beyond the one disciplinary boundary while recognizing that "interdisciplinarity cannot live without the disciplines.... You cannot cross boundaries if you don't know where they are" (Hunt 1). Interdisciplinary practices, at the same time as they challenge disciplinary conventions, also, paradoxically, depend upon them in the same way practitioners of different disciplines define themselves in relation to each other.

Cautions

There are a number of issues to be aware of when engaging in research of an interdisciplinary kind. There may be difficulty in gaining recognition within departmental structures. Donald Campbell characterizes these structures as involving "tribalism or nationalism or in-group partisanship in the internal and external relations of university departments, national scientific organizations, and academic disciplines" (328).

More recently, Tony Becher has written the book *Academic Tribes and Territories: Intellectual Enquiry and the Cultures of Disciplines* to explore how disciplines operate with bounded ideas about what constitutes recognized "excellence" in a field. Even in university cross-appointments, the promotion and tenure of a jointly-appointed faculty member may be administratively dealt with through one "home" faculty.

There may also be unspoken suspicions on the part of some that anyone who has diverse interests really has not focused their attention, and has a certain lack of scholarly commitment. Lack of firm affiliation with a particular discipline, that is, to be "undisciplined," implies that one has not been subjected to discipline; one is untrained, disorderly, and capricious. From this vantage, to be an interdisciplinarian is to be marginal to the centrality or cutting edge of a discipline, to be, in a certain sense, socially and intellectually "homeless."

Julia Bettinotti asks the key question: "Comment peut-on être compétent dans son domaine et aussi dans d'autres?" (qtd. in Herz 13). How can one be competent in one's own field as well as in others? This question is apt to produce a certain guilt. It can be partially answered, though, through the recognition that to keep up with the ever-growing literature within one field, or one sub-specialty, is beyond the means of any individual. Campbell points out that what is recognized as a "discipline" is in fact a "collective product, not embodied within any one scholar." Each discipline represents "a congeries of narrow specialties each one of which covers no more than one-tenth of the discipline with even a shallow competence" (330).

It is, moreover, as Hunt suggests, "no simple matter to enter into the scholarship of another field" (3). Spatial divisions between departments may preclude easy or informal interactions between faculty. Library classification systems privilege these same divisions. To conduct research may require multiple trips to different libraries, each with its own classification systems and protocol. Consulting, using, or borrowing insights from multiple disciplines can unintentionally offend disciplinary specialists. Oversimplifying, decontextualizing or misinterpreting complex issues, citing methods or concepts of theories out of context, or defining things that may be obvious in one discipline but not in another are all potential hazards. The sense of "being a stranger in a strange land," of learning a new language, of learning how to translate, are no less palpable when contemplating the different citation practices for different scholarly journals. In their description of those who venture outside their own specialization and pursue encounters with the academic "Other," Aiken *et al.* compare the intrepid with "at best ... neophytes— stereotypical tourists who cannot speak the language of the field they presume to visit and who overlook nuances and complexities apparent to the natives; and at worst as dangerous trespassers, or colonizers seeking to expropriate territory not their own" (261).

I, myself, have experienced the following comment from an anonymous reviewer of a paper submitted to a scholarly journal: "It is always difficult to assess the theoretical and methodological substance of a piece that is informed, and in many ways sustained by interdisciplinary research." One obvious way of circumventing this kind of problem of vulnerability to new kinds of criticism is to submit papers to colleagues in different departments to get their reactions.

Strengths

To balance those cautions I have briefly discussed above, the strengths of interdisciplinary approaches to research are ample. Interdisciplinary research answers the ongoing feminist call to re-evaluate and re-calibrate ways in which knowledge is produced. It questions the need to fragment, splinter, and compartmentalize (de-partmentalize) issues. It does not necessarily require a resolution of contradictions, recognizes that closure may not be desirable, and validates multiple perspectives in problem-oriented research. Further, such research leads to a keen sense of reflexivity, and thus an acknowledgment of one's own potential blindness, as well as an appreciation of the insights to be gained from the experiences of others' areas of blindness. I am thinking of the

Indian fable about the blind men who feel an elephant. Each describes the elephant differently, connecting in some way with one part of the elephant's anatomy—its trunk, the leg, the ear, the side, the tail. The fable deals with the interplay between blindness, experience, understanding, memory, and imagination—how we remember what we have experienced, how we represent that experience, and how we communicate that experience to others. If they are articulated, the limitations posed by one's particular kind of blindness, or in anthropological terms, ethnocentrism, can lead to fruitful insights and inspiration.

An important part of the ethical concerns for many feminist researchers is to assure that their work answers a need, in some way a return of the "gift" to those who have offered part of their lives to the researcher (Harries-Jones). The interest many feminist researchers have in actively directing their research to strategic and applied contexts requires a revisioning of the boundaries between the academy and other communities, between formal knowledge and everyday experience. Susan Sherwin suggests that "it is far more urgent to widen the conversation beyond academe than to put our energies into regrouping within the academy" (qtd. in Herz 10).

Leading on from this, questions about "disciplinarity" and "interdisciplinarity," or being "disciplined" and "undisciplined," should be posed with a sense of urgency that precludes limiting discussion to within the safe and conventional bounds of the scholarly, university setting. These questions are bound to the kinds of research we choose to do, and the contributions that research may make to "help" in the broadest sense.

Since I have begun my research on homelessness in Toronto, I have revisited an article written by Sue Estroff, herself an anthropologist, entitled "'Who Are You? 'Why Are You Here?': Anthropology and Human Suffering." Her brief article about doing research, about going away from her everyday world, concerns the questions she was asked when she entered a world "where there were only two reasons and criteria for presence—either you were crazy and needed treatment, or you weren't and provided treatment" (368).

> Why I was there was to witness, experience, understand, and communicate the suffering and despair along with the culture of others who are different from us.... Our task is to *not* become paralyzed by our pain or even disgust when we witness suffering born of incapacity, stigma, or disease. Our task is to *not* look away, mystify, romanticize, and intellectualize, or relegate to resolutions at business meetings the human experiences of those who are

different. We are here (or there) to see, to hear, to describe, to understand, and to make comprehensible these people and their lives to those who *do* turn away. Our task is to *not* get distracted by our own responses to what we see and feel, but to push on, to bring a rich and clear vision to others who *do* look away, or who ignore, deny, or distort what they see. (370)

The kind of research that Sue Estroff is speaking about is the kind that carries the researcher beyond the hallowed halls of academe, beyond the safety of familiar theoretical paradigms, and therefore beyond the familiarity of disciplinary cloaks, beyond, moreover, even conventional understandings of ordered experience, understanding, and memory.

Footnotes

[1]Klein's *Interdisciplinarity: History, Theory, and Practice* provides an extensive and thorough overview of the practices and projects associated with the rubric "interdisciplinarity." The word encompasses an extraordinary diversity, including, "collaborative research, team teaching, hybrid fields, comparative studies, increased borrowing across disciplines, and a variety of ... 'holistic' perspectives" (11).

[2]Van Maanen makes explicit the relationship of impressionist painting to fieldwork: "It is the impressionists' self-conscious and, for their time, innovative use of their materials—colour, form, light, stroke, hatching, over-lay, frame— that provides the associative link to fieldwork writing. The impressionists of ethnography are also out to startle their audience. But striking satires, not luminous paintings, are their stock-in-trade. Their materials are words, metaphors, phrasings, imagery, and most critically, the expansive recall of fieldwork experience" (101).

References

Aiken, Susan Hardy, Karen Anderson, Myra Dinnerstein, Judy Lensink, and Patricia MacCorquodale. "Trying Transformations: Curriculum Integration and the Problem of Resistance." *Signs* 12.2 (1987): 255-275.

Anderson, Rae. "Masks and Women: Challenging Exclusion." Master's thesis. Interdisciplinary Studies, York University, 1988.

Anderson, Rae. "The Corset of Compromise: Negotiating Social and Spatial Boundaries in Two Artists' Housing Cooperatives in Toronto." Doctoral

Dissertation. Department of Social Anthropology, York University. 1993.

Becher, Tony. *Academic Tribes and Territories: Intellectual Enquiry and the Cultures of Disciplines*. Milton Keynes, England: The Society for Research into Higher Education, and Open University Press, 1989.

Campbell, Donald. "Ethnocentrism of Disciplines and the Fish-Scale Model of Omniscience." *Interdisciplinary Relationships in the Social Sciences*. Eds. Mazafer Sherif and Carolyn Sherif. Chicago: Aldine Publishing Company, 1969. 328-348.

Estroff, Sue. "'Who Are You? Why Are You Here?': Anthropology and Human Suffering." *Human Organization* 43 (Winter 1984): 368-370.

Harries-Jones, Peter. "From Cultural Translator to Advocate: Changing Circles of Interpretation." *Advocacy and Anthropology*. Ed. Robert Paine, St. Johns, NF: Institute of Social and Economic Research, 1985. 224-248.

Herz, Judith. *Fields and Boundaries: The Shifting Space of Disciplinarity*. (Round Table, 2 June 1993.) Ottawa: Canadian Federation for the Humanities, 1994.

Hunt, Lynn. "The Virtues of Disciplinarity." *Eighteenth Century Studies* 28.1 (1994): 1-7.

Kavoori, Anandam. "The Purebred and the Platypus: Disciplinarity and Site in Mass Communication Research." *Journal of Communication* 43.4 (1993): 173-181.

Klein, Julie Thompson. *Interdisciplinarity: History, Theory, and Practice*. Detroit: Wayne State University Press, 1990.

Stember, Marilyn. "Advancing the Social Sciences through the Interdisciplinary Enterprise; Presidential Address." *The Social Science Journal* 28.1 (1991): 1-14.

van Maanen, John. *Tales of the Field: On Writing Ethnography*. Chicago: University of Chicago Press, 1991.

Writing for the Academy
Anxieties and Strategies

Deborah Clipperton
Graduate Programme in Women's Studies, York University

Women have particular problems writing for the academy. I consider myself something of an expert on the topic, since I have worked through two major writing blocks, and I am currently in the middle of a third. I am amused to find that it is much easier to write about writing than actually to write. When a couple talks all the time about their relationship instead of having one, they are engaging in one of the solipsistic jokes of postmodernist culture, having a relationship about a relationship. Here, I am writing about writing. Instead of writing.

Writing is a topic of great interest to writers. Over the centuries almost every writer sometime in his or her career has written about writing, either to discuss the painful creative process or, for English writers at least, to express despair about the state of the English language. I want to tackle it from a practical, personal, and feminist perspective. And I want to suggest, without being essentialist, that some women have problems writing that are particular to their gender. For this reason, it is important for us to search out particular solutions to those problems.

There are some dangers in the statement that woman suffer writing difficulties because of their gender. I do not think this is because of any inherent difference in capacity. It is, I think, because we are writing in the context of a patriarchal culture. Even those of us who have carved out a niche in Women's Studies, and feel somewhat protected from the more drastic exigencies of male dominance, encounter the patriarchy. Even when we are alone in front of the keyboard, engaged in the very private experience of writing, we encounter patriarchal values as they have shaped our ideas and our psychology. Obviously, by now my thoughts have been as informed by my feminism as they initially were by my experience of male dominance.

One of the dangers of identifying the patriarchy as one of the sources of our writing difficulties is that the problems will appear insurmountable, and we will be overwhelmed and discouraged. Looking the dragon in the face can be terrifying. Equally, we do not want to identify ourselves as victims. The situation is much more complex than that. Patriarchy is not real like a chair, or a person. Rather, it is a power structure, a system of thought. Women never engage the patriarchy directly, but are in relation to it; often this is a relation of resistance. In many ways, the word "patriarchy" is not as useful as it once was, and has fallen out of fashion. I, for one, however, do not want to lose the word, lest we lose the concept. When women write, I believe, we encounter the patriarchy, externally and internally.

To me, feminism is the attempt to theorize this encounter, and so, sometime in the course of their careers, feminist writers must think about writing as a political act, a revolutionary act, an act that ruthlessly examines oppression as it exists in the language that we use every day. Since our ideas are formed out of language, this has been a crucial area of feminist investigation. This is the principle behind the feminist surge towards gender neutral language and only one example of how language is a tool of politics. Great thinkers have dealt with this at length, of course, but I will only say here that the construction of language constructs thought. If we have no language for it, we cannot think it.

I am interested in examining the internal encounter with the patriarchy as it impacts on Women's Studies students writing for the academy. Over and over again, women have told me about feelings of anxiety and fraudulence that manifest in various ways, affecting their work habits and even their health. I have heard stories of writing blocks, procrastination, time management problems, insomnia, anxiety attacks, weight gain, headaches, stammering, bowel problems, and other disorders. Obviously people's quality of life is being affected. If the root cause is an internalized conflict with patriarchal values, then the solution must be both political and psychological. On a political level, we must do what we can to change the value systems that confine us. Women are working hard to do that both through political praxis and pedagogy, but we must also continue writing in the face of it. Somehow, we need to get to that moment of sitting down alone with the blank page.

Years ago I heard a radio interview with Erica Jong. She said that she never sat down to write without facing terror; that every moment she sat in front of her computer she was afraid; that in her career as a writer, her main task was to find a way of putting the fear aside so she could write. I was in the middle of my first experience of a writing block when I heard this, and was greatly reassured to hear a woman writer describe what I was experiencing myself. At the time, not many women were talking about the problems they were having writing for the academy, and how those problems were gendered. Jong suggested that every time a woman sits down to write, she is breaking a primary social taboo. Women under patriarchy are to be silent, chaste, and obedient— seen, but not heard. Whenever we write, we break this rule. Whenever we publish, we challenge dominant definitions of femininity. This has been particularly true of women writing as essayists. Novels and poetry are more acceptable feminine literary forms, residing as they do in the province of intuition and imagination. But women writing to demonstrate and share knowledges that have historically been associated with the masculine have had to give up aspects of their identity to do it.

This theory suggested to me that there were identity issues at work in my own writing block. What we call a writing block is a *thinking* block, a block in the flow of ideas. I was sure that the reason I could not write was that I did not have anything to say. As a student, the one thing I can never afford is having nothing to say. Just not bright enough, I thought; I was actually on the verge of quitting school. The notion that I was blocked because something was blocking me, that something *outside* me was now *inside* me by virtue of a process of identification, this was very liberating.

Following Jong's remarks about fear, and my own thinking about femininity and the literary form, I decided that if I was afraid to write essays because it meant giving up my identity as a woman, I would try poetry. What I wrote gave me an understanding of what I was up against in my own psychology.

This is what I wrote:

Girls Don't See Rats, Part I

Girls don't see rats.
It's a known fact,
although they run from coffee to candles,
inside conversations, under everything that moves,
girls don't see rats.

With that dark knowledge, it is feared,
we could not adequately love,
and floors would go unwashed
if we saw rats.
But I, before they were named to me
and then the name forbidden,
saw them as dark shapes with quick running beats,
blowing yellow breath
and stinking loudly like a Panama shirt.
I'm thinking of marked cards and bullets now;
these are forbidden thoughts;
structured forbidden by the nuances of language
as I first learned the categories of experience.
Some had words, others disappeared below;
the rats, below; girls don't see rats.
They haunted my dreams for years, a knowledge unknown,
lurking like some sixth dimensional demon,
but graphically depicted, like the swamp thing,
or wolverine, but outside time;
I couldn't remember precisely, once I woke,
the shape or sound,
but only how it felt in those dark corridors.
Starlight on its way to us is bent
by the huge gravitational pulls of a black hole,
like water, diverted by a rock in the stream bed,
it curves around, continuing on its way
and the enormity remains unseen.
It was like this with me and the rats.
My thoughts and memories bent around them.
They were detectable only
by how they affected other thoughts,
whose colours were shifted by those unseen forces.
And so in my thirties, I came up against a huge stone wall,
yellow with age and crusty with lichen.
Thou shalt not see rats, it said,
and there was no way over or through.
I could not write a single word,
by now there were too many anomalies.

This is a poem about forbidden knowledge and how it is gendered. I was born in 1952, into the thick of the American Dream. The gender dynamic was intense; girls did some things, boys others. Girls did English and history, boys did science and learned chess. The family constructed an appearance of normality that it worked very hard to maintain, and gender dynamics were the stuff of that pretense. Even as a little girl, I knew that all was not as it seemed. But knowledge of dark things, knowledge of the way things worked, that was something girls did not talk about. It was okay to know about it, girls could know things, but you had to keep it to yourself, lest you lose your place. And femininity is your place. As an adult, it was acceptable for me to know things, but not to demonstrate it publicly, and especially not to write.

The fear I encountered when I sat down to write papers about how things work, papers that lead toward a degree, papers that address gender dynamics and male dominance and class and race and the lies and deeds that get the rich richer and the poor without voice, and that keep little girls from saying they know about the rats, that fear was based in reality.

We are engaged in Women's Studies in exposing oppression. This is very anxiety-producing. In addition, we are women producing knowledge and going public with it. It was very important for me to hear another woman speak with great feeling of her fears around writing. It helped me to name my own. I needed to switch out of the essay form in order to identify my own specific fear. But having identified it, how then to hold it in abeyance so I could write?

I spoke recently with Jan Geddes, publisher of Cormorant Books, a small, notable house in the Ottawa area. Geddes reads a thousand manuscripts a year. By far, the majority of completed manuscripts she receives are from men. From women, she tends to receive manuscripts in progress. When I asked how she explained that difference, she said she thought that women, in their writing process, often reach a point at which they need and ask for affirmation. They need to hear that the project is of value and find it difficult to proceed without that positive connection.

Daniel Stern, a noted psychoanalytic theorist who synthesized years of baby-watching in a comprehensive theory of infant development, stated unequivocally in his book *The Interpersonal World of the Infant* that learning takes place in the context of a relationship. Development is not about a process of separation and individuation towards an autonomous self, but about developing the capacity to relate interpersonally. Even when we are alone in front of the keyboard we are in a cultural and interpersonal context. We bring our demons with us. Why, then, should we not seek out friends and allies to take there too?

I was able to admit I was suffering from a writing block because I heard another woman talk about it. I was able to work out its meaning by talking about it with my therapist and with friends. For a while, I gave my relationship to writing as much import and attention as I gave my sex life. I brought my writing and my fears about writing into my relationships and I used my relationships to help me deal with my fear. Establishing a good connection with my teachers and fellow students has been important for me. I needed to recognize that I write comfortably in the context of a relationship. I need to be writing for someone I know is going to read what I have written.

I find it interesting that in the few years that York University's Graduate Programme in Women's Studies has been in existence, women have been organizing themselves into groups to support each other as they proceed toward their degrees. Study groups to prepare for comprehensive examinations, seminar groups, and writing groups are forming as women recognize and normalize their need to talk about their intellectual work. Recognizing this need for affirmation and connection has allowed women to begin to give each other context, to write for each other.

Each of us has our own way of dealing with fear as we feel it in the moment. I speak as a psychotherapist when I say that the way to deal with fear is to recognize it and sit with it. You cannot block fear without blocking everything else. But it is much easier for me to sit with my fear if I have my teachers and fellow students sitting with me. It is crowded at my keyboard now.

Apart from all this, there is an inherent tension within writing, independent of a writer's psychology, an occupational component that anyone faces, a resistance within the form itself. The standards that have been set throughout history are so high, that to write means putting yourself on the playing field with the greatest players. How is it possible to write a scholastic paper of any merit with a thinker like Foucault hovering over your shoulder? How does a playwright even begin to write a play with Shakespeare in the background? How can a poet who has read Emily Dickinson bear to set pen to paper? Has not Virginia Woolf said it all? What about Susan Sontag, Annie Dillard, Rachel Carson, Judith Butler, and so on? These are giants, we read them daily. With them in mind, a certain careless courage is required when we take the playing field with these competitors.

Furthermore, the distance between the idea of a text and the finished work is enormous. It is very difficult to sit down with an idea, contain the enormity of what needs to be done, and write, one line at a time, through to the end, without getting overwhelmed and anxious somewhere along the way. It is sometimes helpful to suspend judgment for the first draft, to become careless of the quality of the writing, to remember that what is important is the re-write. Even the worst writing can be made better in the second draft.

It is inherent in the form that we always fall short of an imaginary ideal, whether it is set by precedent, or by our own conception of a finished product. Every line falls short of this ideal. Every completed piece is a disappointment. A writer witnesses this confrontation between the imagination and reality. It creates a kind of inertia, a drag on the impulse to create and to express a thought. Often when writers encounter this resistance in the form, they think there must be something wrong with them, that they do not have enough courage, or talent, or self-respect to be a writer. In fact, it is a component of writing that we must willingly take on. All of us have the right, if not the obligation, to give voice to ideas.

References

Daniel Stern. *The Interpersonal World of the Infant: A View from Psychoanalysis and Developmental Psychology.* New York: Basic Books, 1985.

Praxis

Team-Teaching Women's Studies

A Graduate Student Perspective

Jennifer Lund and Katherine Side
Graduate Programme in Women's Studies, York University

This essay analyzes, in the context of our own learning and professional development as graduate students, our experiences of and reflections on team-teaching an introductory Women's Studies course. Our reflections emerged from our conversations about feminism, feminist pedagogy, and the Women's Studies classroom, while we team-taught the course and a year later. They have been further enhanced by two sets of classroom evaluations and a peer evaluation. In this essay (originally given as a joint oral presentation) we set the context for the course, discuss how our understandings of feminist pedagogy informed our design and delivery of the course, make some personal reflections on the process, and raise questions about team-teaching in general.

Setting the Context

Our team-teaching experience took place in a second year, interdisciplinary "Introduction to Women's Studies" course. It was a 13 week evening course, two evenings a week in the summer of 1994, through Atkinson College, York University. Atkinson College offers university courses mainly for the mature university student. The 35 students in our course were all women. Roughly half were mature students; all were working on various stages of undergraduate degrees. At the time that we taught the course we both had completed our second year of PhD studies in the Graduate Programme in Women's Studies at York University and were preparing for comprehensive examinations.

As students and as teachers we brought different experiences, backgrounds, skills, and knowledge to the course. Jennifer had taught anthropology courses at an Ontario university and had been a member of teaching teams in anthropology and Women's Studies at two other universities; Katherine had been a member of a teaching team for an introductory level university course in Women's Studies for three years previously. Our backgrounds in anthropology, history, and literature, and in physical education, anthropology, and Women's Studies respectively, gave us the confidence to structure an interdisciplinary course.

Course Design and Delivery

We made a conscious attempt to expose students to a wide variety of course materials. We derived course materials from academic texts, journals, literature, poetry, plays, and videos. Course materials were selected from Women's Studies, sociology, history, literature, popular culture, and anthropology. Some members of Atkinson College's Women's Studies faculty, and students in the Graduate Programme in Women's Studies, provided guest lectures, and The Linden School, a local feminist day school, performed a play for our class.

We both taught material that was within and outside of our own "traditional" academic backgrounds and training. The presence of another instructor in the classroom alleviated fears about potential "classroom disasters" in "experimenting" with relatively new areas or areas in which we felt "inexperienced."

With the encouragement of Atkinson College faculty members we incorporated our own areas of interest into the course. Despite our initial reluctance about whether our research would be of interest to others, we soon recognized the benefits of including our own work. Including our research interests made us feel confident, and competent, as teachers. It added previously unforeseen dimensions to our work, and allowed us to share our enthusiasm about our topics. In discussions students brought up points that we had not previously considered. They highlighted assumptions that we had overlooked as well as reinforcing some of our thinking.

Pedagogical Considerations

Throughout our teaching, and in preparing to write this essay, we read and discussed feminist pedagogy and the Women's Studies classroom. We recognized that power relations existed in our classroom, as they do in all classrooms. While we consciously tried to create a space for discussion, dialogue, and debate, we realized that issues of silence and discrimination are complex and multifaceted. Negotiating authority with the students was also complex. At times we felt anxious lecturing to such a bright group of students, to whom we often seemed closer than to our own professors.

We recognized that the model often held up as an ideal model of learning is one that is less teacher driven, and we acknowledged that it is difficult to implement, even by the most experienced of teachers in the Women's Studies classroom. We nevertheless tried, and experimented with various methods of teaching and learning, some more successfully than others. We blocked a large amount of classroom time for guided small group work and discussions so that students might more freely contribute among themselves to the dissemination of knowledge in the classroom. We varied the traditional lecture format, sometimes starting the class with group work that we then used to guide a lecture that followed. We began a section on motherhood by letting students identify and discuss themes that emerged from a selection of poems about mothers and mothering, and we later reflected on how the themes they identified have been explored and considered in relation to feminist scholarship.

Personal Reflections: Katherine Side

We learned from teaching, and writing this essay that while collaboration can be time consuming and generally a slower process than working on our own, there are also benefits. Our experience reinforced my understanding that teaching is about learning.

Integrating Our Own Work

I benefitted from including my work on women's friendships with women. I introduced the topic by citing a passage from Virginia Woolf's *A Room Of One's Own* about Chloe and Olivia, two women who share a laboratory: "Chloe liked Olivia... Do not start. Do not blush. Let us admit in the privacy of our own society that sometimes these things happen. Sometimes women do like women" (Woolf 89). I included the discussion of women's friendships with women in a unit on family, as a challenge to its monolithic constructions and to illustrate ways in which women's friendships have been included and excluded from considerations of family. Later, students maintained on an examination question that the topic of women's friendships with women had been considered solely in the context of sexual preference. This alerted me to ways in which sexuality is constructed as a defining issue in women's friendships and provoked my own thinking about how this limits full consideration of women's friendship relations in feminist theory and practice.

Jennifer and I worked hard in our lectures to emphasize why we favoured certain texts and approaches to them, why we lectured on what we did, and how it related to course aims. It was at times difficult to gauge the students' understanding of complexity while at the same time not overwhelming them.

Working Collaboratively

Our collaboration provided an opportunity to share resources and knowledge and to acquire feedback on content, scope, methods, and interpretation. Teaching with someone else opened up texts and approaches that we might otherwise not have considered. I know that I read material more carefully and understood it more thoroughly when I had someone to discuss it with. Jennifer's enthusiasm for feminist pedagogy and her willingness to experiment with new methods and approaches were contagious, and I benefitted from this.

From the outset we agreed to a collaborative work process. We designed the course syllabus and assignments jointly. On the first evening we presented the course outline together in hopes that students would see, and get accustomed to, our collaboration. We marked the first set of student assignments together, and we shared the presentation of a lecture we wrote together, and on occasion, we co-lectured.

We worked well together, in part because our work processes were compatible (although our software was not) and because of the strength of our friendship. In retrospect, our collaboration also worked well because we came to teach this particular course at the same time, with roughly the same degree of teaching experience and seniority. Neither of us felt she had been "invited" to teach in someone else's classroom, and neither of us had a rigid design for the course, or a previously developed syllabus or reading list that we felt invested in.

My own personal belief in the value of collaboration was reinforced by this experience. Our students generally considered having two instructors a strength of the course, as they noted on our teaching evaluations. Some of them highlighted the opportunity to get to know two instructors and have the input of two individuals as a valuable aspect of the course overall.

Personal Reflections: Jennifer Lund

I would like to address team-teaching as part of my professional development in graduate Women's Studies. Writing two years after we taught the course, I am mortified with how concerned I was with my performance, and my lack of explicit attention to how students were learning. In more forgiving moments I have decided this is a part of learning to course direct, and that my own obsession at the time with authority in the classroom, learning to lecture, and coping with critique was not self-indulgent. I hope this discussion of my experience will be informative for those embarking on their first course directorships.

Authority in the Classroom

Negotiating authority with the Atkinson College Women's Studies Programme, with each other, and with the students raised particular kinds of issues. Being a student, but not a student, being a professor, but not a professor, was a challenging and often difficult role to fulfill. With our students we were professors, but when Atkinson College Women's Studies faculty guest-lectured for us, our role as graduate students also came into the classroom.

We had to work out how we were going to make decisions about the course. Katherine has already noted the ease with which we were able to do this, and I am sure this is not always the case. We talked about negotiating authority between ourselves in our very first meeting. As graduate students, our roles in team-taught courses had varied considerably from course to course. We decided that, despite disciplinary differences between us, we wanted to design a course with a central argument that developed throughout the term. We chose to emphasize the academic and activist implications of theorizing women as a group, without minimizing the ways their experiences are reflected through race, class, and sexual preference. Our emphasis on coherence and consistency may have been overdrawn, but again we thought it was better to have erred in that direction. One Atkinson College professor who guest-lectured for us suggested that we present more debate between ourselves, and in future it is something I will be more comfortable to undertake.

Learning to Lecture

Despite having lectured already, my relative lack of experience meant that I was less willing to provoke and challenge in my solo lectures. While this may be partly my personality, I also believe it is a reflection of a learning process. My biggest challenge was sticking to a central argument in a lecture, and not presenting more than two or three ideas. The urge to direct my lecture to Katherine, and not to the students, was also something I struggled with. I found it much easier to experiment with approaches to group work, an area in which I have more background and experience.

The experiences of lecturing and group work were both supported for me by Katherine's presence in the classroom. She was always there to respond to a point or question on which I was stumped, or direct discussion away from something that was becoming unproductive. While I was confident in my knowledge of the field of Women's Studies, most of my previous teaching had been in anthropology. Katherine's considerable feminist activist background, as well as her experience teaching Women's Studies, added a dimension to the class that I could not provide at the time. It would seem to me, therefore, that team-teaching is essential to any interdisciplinary programme.

Coping with Critique

Coping with critique was greatly enhanced for me by team-teaching. Debriefing after the sessions each evening was extremely important. I could relax when things were going well, and could concentrate on what needed work when it was apparent to both of us that some aspect of the course or classroom was problematic. One drawback of this method for critically ana-lyzing our classroom practices was that I did not keep a journal after each class, as I normally do when I teach. In retrospect, a written record would have been helpful. I have blocked some evenings entirely out of my memory!

It was helpful to solicit and respond to feedback mid-way through the course. We devised an evaluation sheet that asked students what was working for them and what was not. We summarized their responses and talked about what we could work on and what was out of our hands. A critique of my use of repetition in lecturing was valuable in that it pushed me to try out new styles of lecturing. We were able to attribute the workload to curriculum standards of the Women's Studies programme and not overly ambitious personal standards.

In the supportive space of the team I was able to respond to critique and take risks in my teaching. We jointly decided not to use a participation grade. As I had never taught in a course that did not include one, I was concerned this would unfavourably affect the students' final grades. On the first night, students debated the absence of the participation mark, some arguing against and others in support of the marking scheme. We told the students that we would discuss the grading scheme in light of their comments, and after considerable deliberation on our part decided to go with our original grading plan. The students argued they could talk more freely in class without scoring points for the "right" answer. Because we discussed many difficult topics that affect us all, such as violence against women, racism, and homophobia, grading someone's ability or willingness to speak on these subjects seemed unfair and questionable. One student noted on her midterm evaluation that one of the aspects of the course that was working for her was "not having to share." This reinforced my understanding that the Women's Studies classroom is not a "safe" place (a romantic, if not dangerous, myth). While we consciously tried to create in our classroom a space for discussion, dialogue, and debate, I know we also silenced and discriminated against some students.

Many evaluations, however, were also helpful in indicating what did work for students. I have included an anonymous comment from the programme's evaluation form that reflects my concern with professional development for graduate students in Women's Studies: "I thoroughly enjoyed this course and I enjoyed attending each session. Katherine and Jennifer were helpful and I feel that with more experience they will be wonderful teachers (professors)."

Team-teaching also helped me see the value of taking risks in my own area of study. As a feminist ethnohistorian with an interest in personal narratives, one of the most rewarding parts of the course was the response to the choice, on one of our assignments, of interviewing a female family member and writing a brief history of her paid and unpaid work experience. Katherine suggested this project, and had I not co-taught the course with her, I would not have realized how exciting an assignment this could be. In my training as an anthropologist I had been discouraged from interviewing my grandmother for a life history assignment in a field methods course. I still carried with me the lingering suspicion that one could not be "objective" if one's subject was too close to "one." These oral history projects contributed to my understanding of Ontario women's lives throughout the twentieth century. They were as stimulating for me to read as any published accounts of Ontario women's history. The success of this assignment has given me a renewed sense of the "legitimacy" of exploring and writing about my own family history.

As part of my professional development as a feminist academic, the team-teaching experience taught me to trust my own knowledge and encouraged me to expand my horizons, teach new material, and learn from students. It is important to teach what matters to you, what excites you, and what you are most enthusiastic about, while also being open to exploring new subject matter and new pedagogical practices. Being at the same stage in our academic work facilitated our ability to negotiate what we taught, how we taught, and how we evaluated students. But this experience also gave me confidence that I have something to offer when I teach with a more experienced teacher than myself.

Team-Teaching

As Co-Course Directors, we were compelled to think not only about the processes of our learning and teaching, but also about what the dynamics of team-teaching meant to us. Dennis Fox suggests there are various types of team-teaching. He outlines four: the "solo act with eavesdroppers" approach which allows one individual to offer their expertise while other member(s) of the teaching team listen; the "panel approach" which allows all members of a larger team to participate in discussing a particular issue; the "follow your leader approach" which sets up an initial presentation followed by a number of smaller discussion groups around that presentation; and the type we employed, what Fox terms "the double bill," two teachers that share together, in any number of ways, the responsibilities of teaching.

In hindsight, it would have been helpful for us to explicitly ask our students about the dynamics of team-teaching—in what ways did team-teaching, or the particular method of team-teaching that we employed, the double bill, work for them? In what ways did it not work for them? That the dynamic of team-teaching was overlooked by us on both student evaluations seems an interesting point to note. Were we making assumptions about the effectiveness of feminist collaboration? Team-teaching allowed us as teachers and students to explore pedagogical ideas and put them into practice. We were able to share the workload, stay on top of course materials, and develop our confidence as teachers in the context of a supportive environment. We believe our collaborative emphasis in the course on breaking down disciplinary boundaries contributes to the rapidly developing field of Women's Studies.

References

Fox, Dennis. *Team-Teaching in Higher Education*. Ed. R. G. Farmer. Birmingham Polytechnic on Behalf of the Standard Conference on Educational Development Publications Committee. Paper #11. n.d.
Woolf, Virginia. *A Room of One's Own*. London: Harper Collins, 1977.

"Isn't Just Being Here Political Enough?" Feminist Action-Oriented Research
A Challenge to Graduate Women's Studies

Jacky Coates, Michelle Dodds, Jodi Jensen
Women's Studies Department, Simon Fraser University

As three MA students in Women's Studies at Simon Fraser University, we organized a workshop on feminist action-oriented research at York University's conference, *Graduate Women's Studies: Visions and Realities*. Our aim was to present our own struggles to combine activism and academic work, in order to encourage women to share perspectives and visions of activism, and strategies for overcoming institutional and individual barriers. Both our workshop and this essay were developed collaboratively, as we worked through the many challenges involved in blending three distinct voices. Two of us are conducting research which involves participants, while one does research which is theory-based. Consequently, activism takes on different meanings for each of us. In this light, our essay is not intended to be monolithic, and we hope that what follows will spark new ideas and further dialogues among readers.

Whose Vision, Whose Reality? An Introduction to Our Project

Succinctly, the point is to change the world, not only to study it.
—Liz Stanley

We decided to focus on action-oriented research because of our experiences as graduate students in Women's Studies struggling to integrate our academic and our activist ways of being in the world. Rather than pursuing a graduate education in another discipline or choosing not to attend graduate school at all, each of us came to work in an MA programme in Women's Studies for unique reasons. Our reasons have in common the desire to bring our academic research in line with our political and social commitments, to further knowledge about women's lives, and to chip away at multiple oppressions. We have each found in our own ways that being a graduate student in Women's Studies assumes a standpoint which is problematic, and that it is more difficult than we had ever imagined to bring our visions of activism in line with the realities of graduate education. Attempting to incite social change in the context of an institution dedicated to the reproduction of the status quo is "crazy-making," as we are obliged to follow the same rules we simultaneously try to break. Sadly, we have discovered that what becomes important, even in feminist academic life, is success in course work, a scholarly thesis, competition with colleagues for scarce resources, and rapid degree completion to advance promptly through higher ranks in the university.

We organized our workshop as a forum where women who find themselves in contradictory positions in academe could reflect on the relationship between activism and academic work in order to shift our work and the university climate "back to" or "on towards" politics. At the beginning of the workshop we introduced ourselves and explained some of what brought each of us to reflect on the meaning of our work in the university. We expressed our concerns that activism occupies a minimal presence in Women's Studies departments, and our commitment to make every effort to strengthen activism in universities. We talked about what we mean when we use the term "feminist action-oriented research" and indicated ways in which research can make real contributions to social justice.

What is Feminist Action-Oriented Research?

We have defined feminist action-oriented research as research that is designed to allow people to both understand and change inequitable distributions of power, knowledge, and resources with the intention of contributing to anti-oppression movements. It is research for, by, and with communities rather than research *on* communities.[1] A feminist action-oriented project is characterized by being broadly accessible. This may mean that the research results are written in accessible language; it may also mean that the results are made available to its audiences in more than one way. Feminist action-oriented research gives back to communities through concrete measures. It involves a process of interactive theory-building which avoids imposing researcher-defined frameworks (Lather 56), and means that the researcher or collaborative research team is reflexive at every step of the project and prepared to alter the process when necessary. If the action research is participatory, it will include reciprocity with participants as a key feature. Feminist action-oriented research does not produce a final product; rather, it conceptualizes a continuing process whereby new questions are constantly raised. In this way, an action research project can stimulate change and growth in communities, policies, participants (including the researcher), and new research projects. A research project is never an end in itself.

To be more specific, feminist action-oriented research may: forge links between communities, including academic communities; use non-academic language; be published in popular presses; be distributed through community groups; be acted out in popular theatre; redefine what counts as knowledge and what counts as theory; involve collaborative or participatory research strategies; or undertake research by invitation, in other words, at the request of a particular community.

The concept of "action research," as we use it, is intended to be distinguished from its original use by social psychologist Kurt Lewin. Lewin developed the concept in the context of a study during World War II in which he attempted to convince middle-class housewives to purchase less expensive cuts of organ meats. His work has been criticized for its lack of ethics in "the use of group process by persons in power to persuade the citizenry ... to modify their behaviour, under the guise of democratic egalitarian discussion, leadership, and decision making" (Rosenwein and Campbell 125).

The origins of this concept alert us to the dangers of the researcher deciding which subjects need to take action, on what issues, and in which ways. As feminists, we aspire to create social change without "telling" people what to do in the name of their liberation. Reinscribing the polarities between knower and known does little to challenge the status quo or work towards emancipation. In contrast, we advocate action research which is responsive to and often takes the lead from communities. We hope to advance a mutually beneficial dialogue between the university and other communities in which we can share skills, resources, and energy in working toward common goals.

The Conference and the Workshop in Action

As we reflected afterwards on the ways in which the workshop unfolded, we began to realize that the conference environment set the tone, to some degree, for what was possible in our workshop. We came to see the climate of the conference as an example of some of the problems in Women's Studies: in particular, a diminishing interest in activism.

To situate our workshop within the body of the conference, ours was almost the only session which addressed the issue of activism in academe. This surprised us—surely we could not be the only ones concerned with relating graduate Women's Studies to social change and the everyday lives of women. Yet aside from a reminder from Sunera Thobani, President of the National Action Committee on the Status of Women, that Women's Studies has a responsibility to fill the gaps left by social programme cutbacks and global economic restructuring, this conference appeared to be solely concerned with "internal" development issues. The sessions focused around questions of programme development, course development, and professional development without recognition of the broader social context of which Women's Studies is a part.

While planning for the workshop, we were able to have many honest discussions with one another about precisely what we are doing in Women's Studies. We were also able to open this dialogue with other Women's Studies graduate students at Simon Fraser University, and found that we are not alone in our frustration about the separation of activism from academic research. We expected that in facilitating this workshop we would meet women who shared many of our questions about the meaning of feminist academic work and who welcomed the chance to develop strategies.

In the workshop, we asked the women to divide into small groups and brainstorm three questions: (1) Letting your imagination go wild, what strategies could you follow to make your research as action-oriented as possible? If action is already integral to your research, what strategies have you used to make this so? (2) How realistic are the strategies you have imagined? How likely are you to be able to carry them through in your current working arrangement? What would allow you to follow your strategies? What obstacles do you anticipate? (3) How can Women's Studies departments encourage graduate students and faculty to do feminist action-oriented research?

We then returned to a large group discussion to consider our ideas about action-oriented research and the obstacles to doing this type of work in an academic setting at this time. Our intention was to elicit strategies for overcoming formidable obstacles and providing direction for the development of graduate programmes in Women's Studies. We were not prepared for the significant amount of resistance this exercise raised among graduate students, undergraduates, and faculty alike.

We found the split between activism and academics in Women's Studies to be far greater than we had imagined. The discussion which our workshop evoked indicated that graduate students, undergraduates, and faculty in Women's Studies are by no means in agreement about whether activism has any place in Women's Studies at all. Although some women in attendance were truly concerned about making links between activism and Women's Studies, it seemed that many who attended really did not know how academic work could be linked concretely with social change. Even more striking, many no longer asked these questions nor cared about the answers. What came most easily in the brainstorming session and took centre-stage during the group discussion were the numerous, arguably insurmountable, obstacles to doing action-oriented research in Women's Studies. As a group, we seemed to be less able to envision the radical social contributions Women's Studies departments could make, less willing to take risks if our reputations, funding, or advancement could be at stake, less willing to consider doing extra work which might benefit women other than ourselves.

Too Much Reality, Too Little Vision

Many of the small discussion groups skipped the question which asked them to imagine ways of doing action-oriented research, and either went straight for the obstacles, or indicated an unwillingness to envision activist research. One reason for this may be that academe has failed to provide alternative research models, and those few researchers whose methods challenge the status quo remain largely invisible.

As the workshop organizers, we came to realize that a gap existed between our own conception of social change and that of many participants. Our own assumptions lead us to seek ways of conducting research that will directly benefit women in their daily lives, particularly those with fewer resources who are most invisible in academe and in conventional research. We observe that many feminists progressing upwards through the educational hierarchy are increasingly focused on influencing the academic community. These women are well able to imagine how their research will impact the production of ideas, texts, and other scholars like themselves. Indeed, this is a scholar's mark of success: to be considered noteworthy in the world of texts.

Yet, the relationship between texts and social change is seldom explored. If confined solely to the world of texts, does the work of feminist academics contribute to concrete social change any more than the work of other academics? Feminists concerned largely with academe may also focus some attention on university politics, and certainly changes to educational institutions are necessary. But what difference do such changes make to the majority of women who presently lack the resources necessary for education? How does warming up the "chilly climate" or revising curricula to include women make a difference to most women outside academic institutions? Considerable resources are spent in order to benefit relatively few women. While it is important to act politically in one's own community, we believe in establishing political priorities according to relative need.

The Personal Cost of Action-Oriented Research

A predominant sentiment expressed in the workshop was that feminist action-oriented research is impossible for three reasons: a) it jeopardizes one's academic status and chances of getting tenure; b) it is too much work to meet university requirements and ethical and political ones as well; c) granting councils do not value activist research and will not support it.

We recognize the tenuous position of both Women's Studies programmes and scholars in universities and colleges. To speak out for any kind of insti-tutional change may have tremendous personal and professional con-sequences—from receiving less funding and being offered fewer teaching opportunities to having one's promotions stymied. Yet, while the founding of Women's Studies programmes involves political vision, commitment, and personal and institutional transformation, many feminist academics are content to find Women's Studies more and more a part of the educational mainstream; in fact, location within the mainstream is often interpreted as an achievement. In this context, it becomes increasingly easy to forget the transformative vision of Women's Studies and instead compete for financial support, recognition, and tenure. Instead of utilizing their access to institutional resources and privileges to benefit activist labour, many feminist academics, predominantly white and materially advantaged, have found a comfortable niche for themselves in the university. Concern over tenure and advancement has sometimes replaced concern over who continues to be excluded by post-secondary institutions. We believe in using our relative privilege to foster social changes that benefit women other than ourselves or those who are "like" us.

Action-oriented research undoubtedly requires more work than research which is not concerned with such issues as reciprocity, self-reflexiveness, and accessibility. Taking time to pursue research with care demands a multiple work load which sometimes carries a personal cost. It may mean that graduate students take longer to finish degrees and publish less frequently. However, if a research process is unethical or politically irresponsible, its potential to contribute to social justice is severely limited.

Sometimes granting bodies will not fund activist research if it undermines the political and ideological platforms of the funding source. While this dilemma illustrates one of the classic contradictions of undertaking feminist research, there are creative ways to manoeuvre around obstacles. Action-oriented research may be disguised and used for people and purposes for which it was never intended. For instance, a professor who applies for and receives a grant to work with First Nations women on a reservation may direct the funding entirely to the women involved to organize their own research project, with little input from the faculty researcher herself. Research is often an essential part of policy and organizational planning outside the university; governmental bodies and community organizations, among others, may support research into timely social issues. Action-oriented research has the potential to foster strong partnerships between Women's Studies departments and communities outside the university.

What if My Research is Theoretical?

One of the most complicated issues relating to feminist action-oriented research is the relationship of theory to activism. Theory is typically viewed as the elaboration of general, complex, and abstract academic ideas—created in isolation and imposed from above. Activism is often interpreted as the converse, where change occurs through group agitation based on solid first-hand experiences. However, theory and activism should not necessarily be seen as so separate from each other—under the term "praxis," theory and practice are combined. As bell hooks explains, while "theory is not inherently healing, liberatory, or revolutionary" (61), it ideally "emerges from the concrete, from my efforts to make sense of everyday life experiences, from my efforts to intervene critically in my life and the lives of others" (70).

Women act and experience, but women also think and make sense of their worlds. Researchers may "dethrone" theory as the product of academic experts by validating as theory those strategies produced by participants in concert with daily experience.

Theory may also be formulated by a researcher without the direct or formal participation of research participants. Many participants at our workshop were conducting research in the humanities, interacting primarily with texts rather than people, and felt themselves to be excluded from the models we proposed for action-oriented research. However, we attempted to expand the definitions of action-oriented research beyond simple interaction with people to include alternative forms of knowledge construction which aim for fundamental social change. Although such research does not include "formal" participants, it should involve other manners of reflexivity: for example, informal exchanges of information and ideas, and popular, accessible distribution of theory in multiple forms. Different communities should be given opportunities to test academically-produced theories against their own experiences and understandings and to offer criticism, affirmation, and revision.

"Isn't Just Being Here Political Enough?"

Some women in the workshop redirected our questions about action-oriented research by raising the point: "If education was a political act in the '70s, why isn't it now?" Our answer is that it depends who you are. The simple presence of a woman in academe is no longer radical in and of itself since women currently constitute 52 per cent of all undergraduate students.[2] However, people who are members of other historically marginalized groups are still under-represented in universities. Whether students or faculty, their struggles help pave the road for others similarly situated as well as challenge knowledge claims which perpetuate systems of oppression.

The political aspects of education have to do with more than just simple presence. The structure of the academy is a web of institutionalized exclusion, and while getting a foot in the door may be seen as a "privilege" for some women, it can also be the beginnings of many further difficulties. Being part of a marginalized group in the university involves constant struggle. Linda Carty explains that for her, "there is little difference between what we experience on the streets as Black women and the experiences we have inside the university" (15). The recent conflicts in political science departments across Canada attest to the widespread racism and sexism perpetuated throughout universities, the voices of dissent from historically marginalized groups, and the backlash of conservatism from the academic establishment.

Our answer is also that it depends what you teach. Education is not a straightforward privilege, nor is the university an executor of political activism when the dominant knowledge forms being taught serve to maintain existing power relationships in the broader society.

Women's Studies programmes, make too little effort to ensure that various cultural perspectives are taught adequately and pay too little attention to intersections of gender with race and class. Change comes at the cost of entering a daily battle with prevailing attitudes of racism, sexism, classism, and other forms of oppression. Women academics pursuing Women's Studies do not necessarily have the desire, nor perceive an obligation, to challenge oppressive systems of thought, or produce research which contributes to social change. In the absence of doing politically challenging work, Women's Studies programmes run the risk of becoming too comfortable for privileged women scholars.

Let Undergraduates Do It

A theme repeated through the conference, including our workshop, was that undergraduate students are ideally suited to conduct research in tandem with community groups. But asking undergraduate students to develop truly action-oriented projects is unrealistic. Undergraduate students have little power within the university hierarchy, and are not able to assume the kinds of risks that may be involved with this research, and usually do not have the time, support, resources, or sometimes the skills to undertake projects that demand as much attention as action-oriented research.

Asking undergraduates to do the action work also pushes the responsibility away from faculty. It minimizes the importance of activism by suggesting that it is only relevant in the beginning years of academic learning. The suggestion assumes that activism is an introductory concept in Women's Studies, that, once understood, can be passed over and replaced by more intellectual and philosophical pursuits. The hesitancy of some faculty to address and actually conduct action-oriented research reveals just how far removed they may be from the needs of women outside of academe.

Let the Community Groups Take the Initiative

Some women who attended the workshop acknowledged the important social and political contributions which could be made by feminist action-oriented research, and expressed the wish for community groups to communicate more frequently with feminist academics. They perceived that such a dialogue could be mutually beneficial and productive and yet did not necessarily want to commit to the extra burden of reaching out to community groups either as individual faculty members or as Women's Studies departments. This is understandable—after all, everyone has enough work; but grassroots community groups are already stretched to the limit with tasks pertaining to daily survival. Community groups and activists have little trust in academe and for good reasons; feminist activists struggled alongside academics to establish Women's Studies programmes, and yet have received relatively fewer benefits. Reaching out to community groups is crucial for the development of Women's Studies and the responsibilities can be divided creatively within departments. Once lines of communication between community groups and Women's Studies departments are established, relationships can build, and dialogue will become easier and less time-consuming. Graduate students and faculty will then be able to identify research projects that "need doing" and negotiate with community groups how this work is to be done. Getting to this point requires a commitment from graduate Women's Studies programmes to initiate and maintain communication lines, and a faith that these relationships are necessary and well worth the effort

Strategies for Researchers and Departments

There is no safe place here; there are, however, many maps of possibility.
—Donna Haraway

We acknowledge that a commitment to action-oriented approaches involves extra work and a burden of risk not assumed for personal gain. This contributes to at least a "double-day" for feminist faculty and graduate students—academic requirements are met and still other work lies ahead in order to practice feminist pedagogy, to be active in other communities, or to be politically responsible in one's research practice.

Our workshop did not produce much in the way of strategies, so consumed were the participants with reasons why action-oriented research is not feasible. The three of us, however, have engaged in many brainstorming sessions to imagine various ways of doing action-oriented research in a university environment and the structural changes necessary within Women's Studies departments to carry out such projects. We would like to share some of our constructive ideas in the hope that it will inspire others to continue strategizing about research and programme development.

Some Recommendations for Graduate Women's Studies Programmes

(1) Graduate Women's Studies programmes can develop a practicum component in which students find ways of making their work relevant to women's lives by using their skills to participate in activist work, such as teaching outside university classrooms. While departments may not wish to make a practicum mandatory, efforts should be made to avoid "streaming" students towards either an academic or a community work track; this would serve to reinforce the dichotomy between academic and activist work rather than working to blend the two.

(2) Efforts can be made to stretch the limits of what is acceptable to academic tradition and set precedents for creative, alternative research forms. As examples, graduate students could produce a documentary video or popular theatre piece in place of a written thesis, write a series of newspaper articles in lieu of an academic paper, or undertake team research for credit. Faculty and students can share the responsibility for stretching the boundaries of tradition, but it must be recognized that faculty have more power and thus more responsibility to do this work; the support and initiative of faculty are essential. Once precedents have been achieved, incoming students must be informed that they have choices as to what forms their research may take.

(3) Graduate Women's Studies programmes can take the initiative to structure workshops or courses on feminist pedagogy for faculty members, sessional instructors, and teaching assistants, so that our teaching can itself be a liberatory act (hooks).

(4) Women's Studies departments can keep in touch with governmental bodies which administer research funding for studies on "women's issues," social services, health, the environment, and related areas so that graduate students can do research where research is needed and possibly have funding provided to do it. Graduate Women's Studies programmes should also have a communicative relationship with community groups that may request graduate students to do research with them.

Some Strategies for Individual Researchers

(1) By conducting research on topics currently in the media, such as the impact of NAFTA on women, graduate students have opportunities to contribute feminist analyses to public debates. However, many topics not

visible in mainstream media and research are nonetheless crucial to social justice movements.

(2) Sending participants the transcripts of their interviews and focus group sessions contributes to their role in creating theory for research projects. Noting the discrepancies between participant and researcher analysis helps to avoid misrepresentation and appropriation of ideas.

(3) Graduate students can work with community groups over the course of their research process, interacting with people who either live the experiences in question or activists in these areas. This is an essential dimension of action-oriented research, regardless of whether the involvement is a direct research partnership or an indirect means of learning, sharing information, and being active in one's subject area.

(4) Graduate students and faculty can speak jointly with community activists at rallies, film presentations, or political events to encourage links between the university and the broader community. Researchers may also join committees which address political issues pertaining to their research.

(5) Once an action-oriented research project is complete, it is essential to spread the word through as many avenues as possible. There are many options for sharing study results with diverse audiences, including using the media (news, radio, television), writing articles for community newspapers and magazines, distributing study results to appropriate community groups, public speaking, and publishing a book in popular presses.

Conclusion

Our workshop and this paper were developed by group collaboration at every stage, resembling in many ways the type of work we have suggested formalizing in the structure of graduate Women's Studies programmes. Our deliberations provided us the opportunity to share our action-oriented research strategies and to realize how action-orientation can be a central research consideration, regardless of topic and methodological focus. Doing action-oriented research means addressing different issues and raising different questions for each one of us, and ultimately takes on unique shapes in our respective MA projects. Our experiences with the conference have reinforced our concerns about declining interest in activism among feminist academics. We see this decline largely as the result of institutional barriers, such as misallocation of resources, competition, and academic traditions built on exclusion, hierarchy, and individualism. In response, we offer concrete suggestions for feminists committed to navigating obstacles, removing barriers, and bringing their politics in line with their academic work. Graduate Women's Studies programmes need to be responsive to diverse groups of women both within and outside the university, and to provide a structure for graduate students to learn to do the same.

Footnotes

[1]In this essay we refer to communities as groups outside of academe in order to stress the need for Women's Studies programmes to sometimes take a step back in terms of maintaining control over research topics, research methods, and research outcomes. Women's Studies also needs to acknowledge the work done by feminist activists outside the university by sometimes taking a step forward in terms of offering financial support and access to other resources. Ultimately, the goal for action-oriented research is to make connections between university communities, and communities outside academe.

[2]While women enter undergraduate programmes in equal numbers to men, their drop-out rates are higher at each level of the academic hierarchy, such that fewer tenured faculty are women. In addition, women's participation continues to be severely limited in specific traditionally male-dominated fields (Statistics Canada).

References

Carty, Linda. "Black Women in Academia: A Statement From the Periphery." *Unsettling Relations: The University as a Site of Feminist Struggles*. Ed. H. Bannerji, *et al*. Toronto: Women's Press, 1991.

Haraway, Donna. "The Promises of Monsters: A Regenerative Politics for Inappropriate/d Others." *Cultural Studies*. Eds. L. Grossberg, *et al*. New York: Routledge, 1992.

hooks, bell. *Teaching to Transgress: Education as the Practice of Freedom* New York: Routledge, 1994.

Lather, Patti. *Getting Smart: Feminist Research and Pedagogy Within the Postmodern*. New York: Routledge, 1991.

Lewin, Kurt. "Forces Behind Food Habits and Methods of Change." *Bulletin, National Research Council* 108.35-65 (1943): 270-288.

Rosenwein, Robert E., and Donald T. Campbell. "Mobilization to Achieve

Collective Action and Democratic Majority/Plurality Amplification." *Journal of Social Issues* 48.2 (1992): 125-138.

Stanley, Liz. *Feminist Praxis: Research, Theory, and Epistemology in Feminist Sociology*. New York: Routledge, 1990.

Statistics Canada. *Women in Canada: A Statistical Report*. Ottawa: Industry Canada, 1995. Catalogue no. 89-503E.

Whose Direction? Whose Mainstream?

Controlling the Narrative and Identity of Women's Studies

Mary Evans
Centre for Women's Studies, University of Kent at Canterbury

The purpose of this essay is to suggest some problems related to the control of academic narratives: in this case, the narrative is that of Women's Studies, and the context is that of the changing nature of higher education in the West. To be more precise it is my concern (and I hope that of others reading these essays) that the voice which women have slowly, painfully, and with great effort acquired within the academy may be forced or constrained or persuaded to articulate only those ideas which are deemed appropriate to the increasingly managerial interests and priorities of the university.

In just these few sentences, it may have become plain that I do not regard the academy or the university as a "sealed" ivory tower. I very much doubt if any university has ever been anything like an ivory tower, with all that description implies in terms of fragility and separation. Historical evidence suggests something rather different: that universities (certainly in Europe) were always rather robust, and indeed combative places. No doubt there were frail scholars working on issues of detail and preoccupied with questions of intellectual life. But for all these (literally) fellows, there were others perfectly prepared to enter into contemporary debate and more than fully engage in every known form of hedonism and worldly preoccupation. Indeed, before moral seriousness overtook the British universities in the late nineteenth century, the Althusserian term "site of struggle" could well be exchanged for "site of pleasure."

But the re-ordering of the universities (at least in Britain of the 1880s and

1890s) was brought about because the British state recognized that "higher" knowledge, (and routinized and coherent "higher" knowledge) was essential to the purposes of the technical/rational state. As Britain looked uneasily at the military expansion (and expansion in terms of competence as much as territory) of Germany, so the British state realized the importance of organizing knowledge. The scientific institutes and endeavours brought, ironically, to Britain by a German —Prince Albert—became part of the "new" university, in which students followed courses, took exams, and were expected to study in more or less orderly ways (Hobsbawm).

If all male students at Oxford and Cambridge did not immediately achieve this expectation of order and coherence in their studies (and much biographical and historical evidence suggests the contrary, particularly in humanities subjects, throughout the 1920s and the 1930s) then women students, on the whole, did so (Leonardi). Admitted on terms of grudging concession in the late nineteenth century, women at Oxford and Cambridge worked hard and long to prove that they could outperform their male peers.[1] As is often the case in instances of female achievement, the goal posts were immediately changed to de-value what women could achieve. The terms "swot" and "blue-stocking" became commonplace and were familiarized as "normal" forms of description for women undergraduates (Brittain). Nor were women themselves slow to distance themselves from an academic culture: in Dorothy Sayers's *Gaudy Night* the description of a woman's college suggests that there is something distinctly peculiar (and indeed pointless) about women's intelligence. However good women are as academics, the moral of the story goes, it is men who have the "real" brains and can solve the "real" problems.

The often sad, rather than triumphant, story of women in British universities suggests that women have never had the opportunity to construct an academy in which to define and establish our own voice. Thus I would argue that women have entered not "ivory towers" but institutions explicitly constructed around male interests and participation. On one level, this takes the empirical and material form of institutional organization which assumes a male career pattern and the traditional division of domestic labour. On this level, it is largely appropriate to assume (and indeed continue to assume) that women *literally* will be disadvantaged. We do not need to fear accusations of essentialism here, since it is essentially women who have, and care for, children and other dependents.

But on another level, when women begin to engage with what is taught in universities, divisions between "male" and "female" become more complex, and indeed related in complex ways to issues about rationality, the meaning of science, binary oppositions, logocentrism, and so on. As diverse feminist critics of "conventional" knowledge have pointed out, the relationship of gender to the construction of knowledge is complex, and cannot be assumed to be one of straightforward opposition between male and female. Nor, most observers of the contemporary university would observe, can we simply say of these universities that they represent patriarchy. As everyone who has taught in a university knows, the most common refrain is "it's more complicated than that." That refrain is as appropriate here, in the issue of Women's Studies and the contemporary academy, as it is elsewhere.

Accepting that the history of universities is complex (and not always *simply* to the disadvantage of all women) brings us to the present day, and to a situation in which Women's Studies is now an established part of higher education in the West. Obviously, the term "established" has to be read with care, since although it is generally true to say that universities in certain countries in North America, Europe, and Australasia have admitted Women's Studies as legitimate it is still the case that the recognition is not general, nor (even in those institutions where Women's Studies exists) is institutional provision generous. A general pattern can be seen which is best described as toleration rather than active encouragement, whilst in some countries, resistance is still explicit. Moreover, in the old "Eastern" Europe, which is only just beginning to emerge from an understanding of the social and material world dominated by historical materialism, the very question of gender and sexual difference runs counter to traditions within cultures which have sought to minimize rather than maintain social differences between women and men. (For example, we can see in the work of one of the founding fathers of historical materialism—Friedrich Engels—a determination to construct the state as a surrogate father, rather than do anything so radical as shift conventional expectations about childcare and domestic responsibilities). The "second wave" of feminism, which brought feminism to the academy in the 1970s, was largely initially a movement inspired by the writing of white, western middle-class women. Germaine Greer and Kate Millett were just two of those women with close links to the academy.

But just as Greer and Millett actually left the academy (even though Greer has since returned) they gave to it, and to a generation of students and teachers, a sense that the curriculum could, and should, be changed in order to accommodate both the presence and the interests of women. Courses on women were introduced throughout the West; at first in the humanities and social sciences and subsequently in the natural sciences, women's voices began to be heard. It was a re-making of the academic curriculum which coincided with the explosion of the numbers of the student population. From being elite institutions, attended by a small (and generally male) proportion of the population, universities throughout the West were transformed in the years between 1970 and 1985 into mass institutions. Much of this transformation was fueled by politically impeccable reasons: that governments generally recognized "wastage of talents" arguments and were even (in the case of more liberal governments or secretaries of state for education) motivated by commitments to increased, and more democratic, access. The way to university became more open for many students, and diversity, in terms of the constitution of the student population, was often welcomed. Thus by 1985 most western countries had seen an equalization in participation rates in higher education between women and men undergraduates. The university student was no longer necessarily a young man, but was quite as likely to be a young woman.

These changes must sound only progressive to many readers: what could be better than changing the exclusive nature of access to higher education and opening up its many possibilities to a wider group of people? Certainly, the change has brought immense human rewards to many individuals, not to mention the much enhanced earning power that higher education (even in a period of the increased instability of middle-class labour markets) still brings. But in a world which has also seen the publication of Foucault's work on power and discourse, and a world in which studies of elites still demonstrate (at least in Great Britain) the continued domination of white, privately educated males in positions of power, we have to be slightly skeptical about exactly what kind of progress has been achieved in the context of this apparent democratization. We must consider, in fact, that access to higher education is no longer contested. Nor is—in many cases—the nature of the curriculum. Fiercely contested now are the control of the definition of the value of the individual institution, the particular degree course offered, the autonomy of the academic subject, and the relationship between the institutions of higher education and the state. To take the example of Great Britain is to illustrate exactly how these contests are being worked out. Before 1992, when the government ended the binary divide between polytechnics and universities there was a general, unspoken, assumption that most British universities were of similar quality and had similar interests. Something of a Marks and Spencer standard existed, to borrow a comparison from the private sector. Unfortunately for universities, Conservative governments from 1979 onwards did not just want to borrow similes from private industry, they also wished to import (wholesale, as they say in trade) assumptions about management, efficiency, and what has become known as "quality control." As part of this import from private industry (and clearly once one begins to think in this language, terms derived from business become inevitable) universities became subject to various processes of assessment (of research and teaching, most particularly) which have led to ranking systems between them, and within them. No longer do students "go to university," they now go to "good" universities with "research active" departments. Academic staff who cannot (do not or will not) produce the requisite number of academic publications are deemed "research inactive" and often subject to considerable pressure to resign.

All these changes have accompanied the growth in student numbers. Of the British experience it is now safe to say that more students are having an experience of higher education which is rather more mediocre than a smaller number of students had in the past. In short, more people "have" higher education but it is generally not as good. Moreover, the higher numbers have only been achieved by higher workloads for academic staff and the increase in the casualization of academic appointments. Increasingly, there is considerable reliance on hourly paid staff to teach undergraduates, with fewer tenured appointments being made. Inevitably, the gross under-representation of women as academics (rather than as academic consumers) has not improved within this context. At the time of writing, of all full professors in higher education in the U.K. only four per cent are women.

Given this statistic, it is inevitable that increasing numbers of people ask the question: what exactly happens within the academy that women almost disappear as members of the profession? The answers are generally that academic culture is overwhelmingly "male" in the sense that the networks, professional associations, and managerial positions are all dominated by men. In essays published in 1993 (Evans, *et al.*) a number of women academics identified the informal pressures within the academy which marginalize women; a few years previously Andrea Spurling had produced, for Kings College Cambridge, a report which fluently and convincingly identified the processes of the exclusion of women in higher education. What emerges from these, and other studies, is that the experience of higher education convinces many women, in a way which is as subtle as it is effective, that higher education is not for them. Even though the gradual feminization of some aspects of university teaching can be seen clearly (for example, the academic teaching of law and other vocational subjects increasingly includes significant numbers of women) this process is less the result of a commitment to the appointment of women on the part of institutions than the detriment that academic salaries present to men.

In Britain, therefore, the present situation in universities is one in which more women students gain entry to a system which is increasingly underfunded, and largely controlled by men. One of the interesting aspects of this situation is the relative absence of debate in higher education about the impact of coeducation. For decades, British sociologists of education have agreed about the differential impact of coeducation on girls and boys, and in the sociology of education there is a considerable literature on gender differences and secondary schools. The consensus that emerges from this is that girls do better in single sex schools ("do better" here indicating achieving better academic results) whilst boys do better in coeducation. The academic interests of girls are markedly not those of boys (see Shaw). So powerful is this case that it has allowed all-girl schools to remain as such. Yet to raise the same issue about higher education puts an author on dangerous, and different, ground. The assumption is generally made that somehow, by processes too mysterious to define, all the gendered problems that beset student/teacher interaction, choice of subject, and models of learning disappear once students are in a university and over the age of 18. That they manifestly do not is attested by the growing body of literature, particularly from North America, which documents cases of sexual harassment and sexual bargaining about grading. Even so, the problem is still limited and marginalized—indeed, it is largely sexualized. Therefore what tends to emerge as "the" problem of gender and higher education is the problematic relationship between nubile young women and aging male academics.

This sexualization (and indeed personalization) largely ignores the way in which women in higher education are faced with what is far more daunting than individual (probably isolated) instances of harassment by male staff. What confronts women is a far more complex, and far more difficult to define, set of assumptions about knowledge and the relationship of knowledge to the real world. It is, to put it in terms of manifest over-simplification, the habits, ideas, and values of western culture which women confront—and those values and assumptions are largely drawn from a sexual division of intellectual labour and an access to the construction of knowledge which is highly differentiated in terms of race and gender. There is a poignant exchange in Jane Austen's *Persuasion* in which the heroine Anne Elliot protests against the assumption that women are generally more emotionally fickle than men. She points out that statements to this effect have largely been written by men: "Men have had every advantage of us in telling their own story. Education has been theirs in so much higher a degree; the pen has been in their hands" (237).

This wonderfully vivid statement, "the pen has been in their hands," accurately, if dauntingly, sums up the difficulties which women face in the academy. The literal presence in many degree courses of women-as-subjects (with the possible exception of literature) is often virtually non-existent. To read history, or philosophy, or—until recently—any of the social sciences, it would be rare to come across women either as subjects or objects of study. The universalizing impact of such disciplines as politics, philosophy, and history is such as to reduce women and/or non-white people to the status of outsiders. Over 20 years ago Sheila Rowbotham coined the phrase "Hidden from History" to describe the ways in which the traditional study of history simply did not include women unless they were—by default of male heirs—rulers. Similarly, the western tradition of philosophy had assumed, from the time of Aristotle, that women were not just different from men, but actually inferior in terms of moral and intellectual capacity and judgment. It took the best part of two thousand years for writers such as Carol Gilligan and Carole Pateman to emerge and issue radical challenges to the idea of a definitive model of justice, rights, and citizenship.

It was—and is—the impact of gender within traditional constructions of knowledge that gave (and gives) Women's Studies its cutting edge and its potential for a radical challenge to the conventional academy. Yet two important qualifications have to be made. First, it is incorrect to assume an absolute homogeneity within the academy: men do not necessarily agree with one another, and the fault lines of the academy do not always fall neatly into male and female. Secondly, just as Women's Studies has entered the western academy, so the western academy—and here again I shall use Britain as a particular example—has demonstrated that it is highly porous, and far from consistently able to maintain an independence from outside intervention. Thus just as Women's Studies appears to have achieved a presence in the academy, so the academy changes. The possible implication of this—and one which I wish to explore in the following sections of this essay—is that just as the academy in general is liable to absorb aspects of the external political culture, so too is Women's Studies.

The particular shift in attitudes to the provision of state services is described in Britain as Thatcherism. From her first General Election victory in 1979, Mrs. Thatcher's agenda was to reverse the creeping collectivization of Britain and to shift the inspiration for institutional organization away from a quasi-socialist, and certainly publicly funded, model towards that of the market-place. "Internal markets" were to be the form of organization for schools, the health services, and the social services, with the accompanying expectation that all these services could be run along the lines of conventional private industry. After the second election victory of Mrs. Thatcher at the polls, the universities (relatively immune from intervention in the first administration) began to be more explicitly examined and were found wanting in terms of management and "efficiency." The particular form of efficiency which pre-occupied the government was the ability of universities to produce graduates. By the mid-1980s the low rates of participation in higher education for British 18 to 21-year-olds had begun to attract considerable attention. The cry went up (just as it had done in the late nineteenth century) that Britain was lagging seriously behind its main industrial competitors in terms of recruitment into, and graduation from, higher education. In order to show the endless capacity of history to repeat itself, Germany—at that time West Germany—was held up as an example of a buoyant economy and an equally buoyant set of statistics about higher education participation rates.

Thus government concern about higher education became focused on increasing the numbers of students in higher education. The expansion in numbers was to be achieved without any increase in funding. Universities began to compete for students, and to encourage student admissions. If a course looked popular with students and seemed to promise high levels of recruitment, then the course was acceptable. After a decade of a marginal existence, Women's Studies suddenly found itself, in some institutions, as positively favoured. With some cynicism, university administrators also recognized that, in the absence of seriously interventionist equal opportunities policies, Women's Studies could also provide a gloss of "woman-friendliness" which was often absent from the traditional curriculum.

The above should suggest that the expansion (for such it was) of Women's Studies in Britain in the 1980s was not necessarily accomplished for the purest of academic motives. On the other hand, for women students and women academics the shift towards a "consumer" culture in the universities created more academic and intellectual space than had been conventionally available. The combination of new political and institutional circumstances, and the intellectual impact of the atheoretical theory of "diversity" and "difference" of post-modernism created a situation in which opposition to Women's Studies was both theoretically redundant and institutionally unacceptable. Since the resources directed to Women's Studies continued to be few, and since many women academics continued the traditional female pattern of working selflessly for nothing, academic jealousies were seldom aroused by the presence of this new area of scholarship.

But this brings us to what seems to me to be the crucial problem confronting Women's Studies in the British (and indeed with some qualifications the western) academy: the question of the degree to which Women's Studies can control its own narrative in the context of universities which are increasingly dominated, and indeed in many ways ideologically saturated, by assumptions about the normality and indeed the inevitability of the market economy. Mrs. Thatcher's (and indeed Ronald Reagan's) linkage of the market economy with political democracy and civil freedom was extraordinarily effective. This does not mean that Women's Studies (as a subject area) is in any direct sense opposed to the assumptions of the market economy. Academic feminists have as many different political affiliations as others. But it does mean that what is increasingly taken for granted by many is the idea that as citizens of the West we all live in conditions of freedom, with endless opportunities for choice. Thus for women to assert that women generally do not live in this condition (or live in it less generally than do men) seems to run counter to the general direction of the culture, in which the very concept of constraint appears increasingly anachronistic.

This intersection of Women's Studies and contemporary culture, both within and outside the university, gives cause for concern. In particular, what seems worthy of attention is the impact on academic feminism of shifts from generalized centre-left politics towards more right-wing assumptions. In this context what becomes immediately apparent is the change in the language of feminism from the 1970s to the 1990s. In the 1970s feminists generally used the term "sisterhood." In the 1990s the term is seldom used; it has been replaced by the theoretically pluralistic idea of "difference" and the importance of allowing and maintaining difference. Initially, of course, the idea of "difference" was crucial to feminism since it allowed theoretical and political space both to non-white women and to women's different sexual choices. But at the same time as "difference" allowed women to recognize and respect the differences between them, it brought with it a certain loss of oppositional focus. This shift in politics is not in any sense unique to feminism; in many ways all western societies have become more ideologically pluralistic at the same time as they have become more politically monolithic. Few people would dissent from the view that there is more explicit social toleration for different sexualities and lifestyles now than in, say, the 1950s. Yet at the same time this new social tolerance goes with a decline in explicit political differences. Again, to use the British example: commentators from all sides of the political spectrum have expressed the view that the present British Labour Party has come closer in many ways to the present Conservative Party than any previous Labour Party. What unites the parties, the commentators argue, is the acceptance by the Labour Party of the belief in the market economy. Thatcherism accomplished, therefore, the ideological hegemony of the free market.

Debates about the politics of the British Labour Party may seem a long way from the politics of Women's Studies, but I would argue that this context is crucial to an understanding of the present state-of-the-art. The specific ways in which I would argue we can observe the permeation of academic and/or political debate by the values of the free market are threefold. First, there is an increasing assumption that the values of the market place (of economic competition, individualism, and a manifestly "western" lifestyle) are the absolutes of existence. For women to argue against the acceptance of these values places them outside the ideological mainstream. Second, skepticism about the role of the state as a provider of social welfare has created a situation in which women are increasingly forced to adopt (if they can) free market solutions in order to make good the shortfall in public provision. Third—and here I have no doubt that we should identify the United States as a major source of inspiration—there has been a real (and very effective) equation of corporate success and personal fulfillment. It has now become common to deride the "shoulder pad" '80s, but the culture of success is still manifestly apparent, and is most seductive amongst those sections of the population (and those populations) where either private means or public and community resources are the weakest. It is true that successful corporate women have been portrayed (particularly in films starring Michael Douglas) as sexually voracious and unstable (Demi Moore in *Disclosure* and Glenn Close in *Fatal Attraction* are the two most obvious examples) but the focus of critique in these films is not the social values of the characters—particularly the women characters— but the failure of women to play by the accepted sexual rules. In that sense, the films portray that unspoken sense of women not "belonging" in the world of paid work: the "matter out of place" in Mary Douglas's famous phrase. But whilst we might note the still vivid fear of women in the workplace which these films suggest, we have to note that dream factory films of the corporate workplace are not in any sense subject to criticism or discussion. A neutrality of motive is imposed, I would argue, by the visual impact of stereotypically attractive individuals and the implicit suggestion of achieved pleasure and gratification.

Confronting (not to mention challenging) this culture remains highly complex for Women's Studies. We have to note—with obvious regret if not surprise—that at the Rio de Janeiro summit on the environment President Bush made it clear that he did not regard the North American way of life (or the North American way of life which he wished to assume everybody in North America shared) as negotiable. An absolutely explicit commitment was made to a particular use of natural resources and a culture rich in the production of commodities. Negotiating women's relationships to this commitment is deeply problematic. Most feminists are aware of the concentration of poverty amongst women, and thus women seem the natural allies of those politics most committed to state intervention. Yet at the same time, most women also recognize that state and/or national politics are everywhere controlled by men, and that there is no guarantee that more state intervention will mean more woman-friendly intervention. In any case, it is now widely recognized that the public sphere (and with it public policy) can usually only recognize simplicities in human and social action.

These remarks have strayed far, in some respects, from Women's Studies and the world of the classroom. Nevertheless, it is my strongly held belief that what must be retained in Women's Studies is not just a sense of difference— important as that is—but equally a sense of similarity and the similarity of the circumstance of living in a market economy in the late twentieth century. Old-fashioned even anachronistic as it might appear, I would therefore argue for the constant reiteration within Women's Studies of the context in which we live and work. Part of that context has changed much about the nature of universities, and increasingly geared their function to labour market demands. Recognizing this is a small but crucial step towards recognizing that the universities—which women have never possessed—have porous walls and that the best form of defense against outside intervention is the acknowledgment of this imperfect defense. The second essential recognition is that of pressures in the outside world to collude with managerialism, endorse the values of Anglo-American globalization, and accept the refusal of the legitimacy of those real differences—of politics and religion—which is endlessly sought by global capitalism. A large agenda, but nevertheless one which offers women a unique opportunity to create a real politics of difference and to take control of the narrative of reality.

[1]The account given by Vera Brittain in *Testament of Friendship* is particularly telling on this point.

References

Austen, Jane. *Persuasion*. Harmondsworth: Penguin, 1965.

Brittain, Vera. *Testament of Friendship*. London: Virago, 1984.

Engels, Friedrich. *The Origin of the Family, Private Property, and the State*. Harmondsworth: Penguin, 1985.

Evans, Mary, Juliet Gosling, and Anne Seller, eds. *Agenda for Gender*. Canterbury: Women's Studies Committee, 1993.

Foucault, Michel. *Madness and Civilization*. New York: Vintage Books, 1973.

Foucault, Michel. *The Order of Things*. New York: Vintage Books, 1973.

Gilligan, Carol. *In a Different Voice*. Cambridge: Harvard University Press, 1982.

Hobsbawn, E. J. *The Age of Capital*. London: Weidenfeld and Nicolson, 1975.

Leonardi, Susan. *Dangerous by Degrees*. New Brunswick: Rutgers University Press, 1989.

Pateman, Carole. *The Sexual Contract*. Cambridge: Polity, 1988.

Rowbotham, Sheila. *Hidden from History*. London: Pluto, 1973.

Sayers, Dorothy. *Gaudy Night*. New York: Avon, 1986.

Shaw, Jenny. *Education, Gender, and Anxiety*. London: Taylor and Francis, 1995.

Spurling, Andrea. *Report of the Women in Higher Education Research Project 1988-1990*. Cambridge: King's College, 1990.